You Shall Be Praised

*An interactive and uplifting
40-day devotional journey
through Proverbs 31*

by Jamie De Silvia

*A book for all women,
not just wives and mothers.*

D1607728

Dedication

This book is dedicated to all the women who sometimes think they aren't good enough for God, or anyone else. It is for those who either love Proverbs 31 or want to track down this infamous woman and show her a few things. (Haha, I was in the second category!) May each of you see yourself through God's eyes as you read this book.

Gratitude

Many thanks to my husband, Manny, for supporting me on this writing journey (and every other adventure I've taken). Thank you also to my children: Micah, Tirzah, and Levi, for believing that I could do this again. It's a dream come true to see my words in print, but an even greater thing to be loved the way you love me.

I'd also like to thank my prayer partners (you know who you are) for praying me through every step. Much gratitude to all of the wonderful people who bought my first book and thought it was something special and anointed. Your support means so much to me.

The Image on the Cover

The cover was created using one of my original paintings. More of my artwork can be found on Pinterest, Instagram, or Etsy @JamieDeSilviaArt.

Table of Contents

Before You Begin

You are about to embark on a 40-day journey through one of the most challenging passages of Scripture for women! The Lord showed me many new things as I wrote this book, and they may challenge your previous notions about the Proverbs 31 woman.

In the text, I share some of my own experiences to help you apply the principles of the passage in your own life. I'm no expert, no spiritual giant, and certainly not perfect. I am a work in progress. I want to be real with you in hopes that you can relate to the ideas being taught throughout the verses.

There is no magic in this book—only the opportunity to grow closer and to go deeper with God. It is possible to connect with God and receive personal guidance and encouragement from Him. I write in this book about hearing from God, allowing Him to guide us in making decisions, and learning specific things from Him. If this is a foreign concept to you, I'd like to try to explain it!

I'm going to give an example of what it can be like to hear from God. The comparison isn't perfect, so bear with me, but I think it may help if you are unfamiliar with recognizing the whisper of God in your life.

Hearing from God is similar to the experience of "hearing" a loved one's voice who is not with you at the moment. You may see something that reminds you of them. You might be reminded of something they said or did in the past, and at that moment, you feel close to them even though they might be miles away or have gone to heaven. Perhaps you are not even thinking about them, but something they regularly say will just pop in your head. You hear the person's voice in your mind— it's not audible, but you hear it. It may feel like they've sent you some encouragement or guidance. All of this happens in your mind, in a matter of moments, but it's real.

Because God's Spirit lives within the person who believes that Jesus is his or her Savior, this Holy Spirit can remind a person of things that God or Jesus said in the Bible, or things He has already promised or communicated in the past. His voice can come like a thought popping in one's head, a memory resurfacing, or similar to what one might call intuition. It is usually very quiet and gentle but can also be very persistent. To me, this experience is far more powerful than the example I gave about a loved one, but it is a close example of how I have personally heard His voice.

When you read this book, especially the quotations from the Bible, you may sense a quickening or stir in you that bears witness to the truth of what you are reading. Let that stirring have a voice— it may be God speaking to you. It may seem strange, or you may think it's all hype or nonsense, but I challenge you to allow God to speak to you in your heart, and I hope that you will respond to Him. If you want to know more about having a saving relationship with Jesus, turn to the last section of this book.

You will see this symbol ❀ throughout the book. It indicates a question or an activity for you to expand your understanding of the verses or tangibly experience God's presence. Please give the activities a try, even if you think they are unusual! You may want to use a journal to record your responses and any insights you gain along the way.

This book is designed for you to read on your own, allowing time to develop your spiritual life. The book would also be great for a group! Read on your own and then buddy up with a friend or two to discuss what you are learning and experiencing in your personal time with God. Are you in a Bible study group? Plan to discuss a few days of completed readings at your meeting. The questions will create plenty of discussion during your meeting time together.

Day 1: Have We Been Wrong?

Occasionally, when we try to communicate something, the other party takes it the wrong way. They may receive it in a harsh way when we intend to be helpful or positive. That is a tough spot to be in… to be misunderstood.

Perhaps this is how God feels about Proverbs 31:10-31. If we believe that God inspired all of Scripture, then we also believe that God had a hand in composing this passage. We want to understand what He intended to communicate through it.

Who did God inspire to pen the words of Proverbs 31? Scholars do not agree on whether it was Solomon or his mother. I think the most logical answer lies in between: at the urging of the Holy Spirit, Solomon likely wrote down the things his mother taught him. But did He intend for it to become a measuring stick for women throughout the centuries? Unfortunately, the passage is often taught that way in the church. While on the journey to writing this book, God has shown me that throughout my Christian life, I have been quite wrong about the Proverbs 31 passage.

Questions arise when we think about the purpose of this passage. As I said, some might think of it as a standard for women to live by. Others might think of it as a man's guide to choosing a wife. What God has shown me is that *this is not a mandate for women*. Instead, *it is poetry declaring the glory of womanhood*, meant to edify and lift us up.[1]

❦ Has your understanding of Proverbs 31 leaned more toward a mandate for women or an ode to women?

The question before us is whether or not we can set aside any previous ideas we've had about the verses, and open our hearts to receive the affirmation and affection that God means to convey there. It is written as acrostic poetry, where the first verse begins with the first letter of the Hebrew alphabet, and then each verse follows alphabetically through the passage. The attention to detail here shows such artistry and devotion. Are we ready to dive into this poetic work of affirmation?

Here is a summary of what I believe the Lord is trying to communicate through Proverbs 31:10-31. Take a deep breath, open your heart, and let it sink in:

You, My daughter, are a warrior.
You are valuable.
You are trustworthy.
You are a worthwhile investment.
You are a vessel of My goodness.
You are creative.
You have beautiful feet.
You will rise in the night seasons.
You deserve help.
Your territory will expand.
You are fruitful.
You are strong.
Your work is good.
You are full of My light.
Your mess is My masterpiece.
You are a blessing to others.
You will endure the winter.
Your needs matter.
You are robed in righteousness.
You were made for leadership.
You are gifted.

You are clothed in strength and dignity.
You have a secure future.
You walk in joy.
You are wise.
You are kind.
You watch over others.
You need rest.
You are blessed.
You excel them all.
You are favored.
You are beautiful.
You honor Me.
Your fruit will last.
You shall be praised.

❀ What is your response to this ode to women?

❀ Which of these characteristics of women are a direct reflection of God's character?

✿ Ask the Lord how you have been specifically made in His image. Jot down what the Holy Spirit brings to mind.

✿ Respond to the Lord regarding this insight.

Day 2: Setting Aside Old Ideas

If I'm being honest, Proverbs 31 often triggers old thoughts and insecurities from the years that perfectionism ruled my life. I was initially reluctant to write a book about this passage and feared that I might fall back into old habits of performing, measuring, comparing, striving, and shaming.

Clearly, I had allowed this passage to set up unrealistic expectations for myself. In one period of my life, I was very focused on the woman's duties presented in the passage. During another time, I was hyper-focused on the qualities and values demonstrated by her. In both seasons, I pushed myself to achieve these things to gain value and approval from God and others. I let the Proverbs 31 woman personify all of the unrealistic expectations that I've had for myself over the years.

When God led me to write a book on this subject, He promised to show me a new way of looking at the passage—from His perspective. No more shaming, blaming, and "should'-ing myself with Scripture. It's time to explore this passage with new eyes.

" *Who can find a worthy woman?*
For her price is far above rubies.
The heart of her husband trusts in her.
He shall have no lack of gain.
She does him good, and not harm, all the days of her life.
She seeks wool and flax, and works eagerly with her
hands.
She is like the merchant ships.
She brings her bread from afar.
She rises also while it is yet night, gives food to her
household, and portions for her servant girls.

She considers a field and buys it.
With the fruit of her hands, she plants a vineyard.
She arms her waist with strength, and makes her arms strong.
She perceives that her merchandise is profitable.
Her lamp doesn't go out by night.
She lays her hands to the distaff, and her hands hold the spindle.
She opens her arms to the poor; yes, she extends her hands to the needy.
She is not afraid of the snow for her household; for all her household are clothed with scarlet.
She makes for herself carpets of tapestry.
Her clothing is fine linen and purple.
Her husband is respected in the gates, when he sits among the elders of the land.
She makes linen garments and sells them, and delivers sashes to the merchant.
Strength and dignity are her clothing.
She laughs at the time to come.
She opens her mouth with wisdom.
Kind instruction is on her tongue.
She looks well to the ways of her household, and doesn't eat the bread of idleness.
Her children rise up and call her blessed.
Her husband also praises her: "Many women do noble things, but you excel them all."
Charm is deceitful, and beauty is vain; but a woman who fears Yahweh, she shall be praised.
Give her of the fruit of her hands!
Let her works praise her in the gates!
Proverbs 31:10-31

🌀 Take note of any *direct commands* in the passage and write them here.

🌀 Does the number of actual commands surprise you?

🌀 Do you think there are any unhelpful fIlters through which you have read or viewed the passage?

🌀 Ask the Lord to help you see this passage, and yourself, through His eyes.

Day 3: How Much Can We Take Literally?

While the woman in the text of Proverbs 31 lived in a strongly patriarchal society, she was still a very privileged woman. Her family was quite wealthy and she had servants at her disposal. Wealth gave her opportunities that other women would never have been entitled to. We will try to learn what we can, knowing that some of the ideas will apply to us and some of them may not.

There are references in the passage that seem a world away from our experiences today. When was the last time you spun wool and flax into yarn or thread with your spindle and distaff? We will press into the Lord to gain meaning and understanding from these sometimes outdated references, and turn them into metaphors when appropriate.

The stories of women and how they were treated in the Bible can sometimes trigger negative feelings. Let us be aware of this and ask the questions that need to be asked. Is this how God feels about women? Should men view women this way? Is this what the Lord expects from women? Why did God let these things happen? While Proverbs 31 doesn't show much of the oppression experienced by Biblical women, it can still cause us to object to the narrow role that women played in the Hebrew world. It's okay for you to have strong reactions to some of the verses. Talk to the Lord about it and ask for answers and clarity!

This passage can also appear to value marriage and motherhood far above other things that women are capable of. Whether you are married or not, a mother or not, this book is for you. God has some lovely things to say about women and I believe He wants you to hear them! It took me many years of studying, sifting through archaic ideas, examining my reactions to those ideas, and opening my mind to read between the lines to finally embrace this passage of Scripture. I hope that you will press in to hear what your Father in Heaven has to say about you and your role as a woman in this world.

Read through the verses again:

> *" Who can find a worthy woman?*
> *For her price is far above rubies.*
> *The heart of her husband trusts in her.*
> *He shall have no lack of gain.*
> *She does him good, not harm, all the days of her life.*
> *She seeks wool and flax, and works eagerly with her hands.*
> *She is like the merchant ships.*
> *She brings her bread from afar.*
> *She rises also while it is yet night, gives food to her household, and portions for her servant girls.*
> *She considers a field and buys it.*
> *With the fruit of her hands, she plants a vineyard.*
> *She arms her waist with strength, and makes her arms strong.*
> *She perceives that her merchandise is profitable.*
> *Her lamp doesn't go out by night.*
> *She lays her hands to the distaff, and her hands hold the spindle.*
> *She opens her arms to the poor; yes, she extends her hands to the needy.*
> *She is not afraid of the snow for her household; for all her household are clothed with scarlet.*
> *She makes for herself carpets of tapestry.*
> *Her clothing is fine linen and purple.*
> *Her husband is respected in the gates, when he sits among the elders of the land.*

She makes linen garments and sells them, and delivers sashes to the merchant.
Strength and dignity are her clothing.
She laughs at the time to come.
She opens her mouth with wisdom.
Kind instruction is on her tongue.
She looks well to the ways of her household, and doesn't eat the bread of idleness.
Her children rise up and call her blessed.
Her husband also praises her: "Many women do noble things, but you excel them all."
Charm is deceitful, and beauty is vain; but a woman who fears Yahweh, she shall be praised.
Give her of the fruit of her hands!
Let her works praise her in the gates!
Proverbs 31:10-31

❧ Do you have any questions about any of the verses? Jot them down.

❧ Does anything rub you the wrong way? Make note of that here.

❀ Talk to the Lord about these objections and questions. Ask Him to give you some insight along the way.

❀ Take a moment to open your heart and mind to any new truths the Holy Spirit may want to teach you throughout this 40 day devotional.

Day 4: You Are a Warrior

Who can find a worthy woman? {Proverbs 31:10}

Even though Proverbs 31 was written well over two thousand years ago, the fact still holds: women following hard after the Lord make up a small percentage of the population. Who can find a worthy woman? You are a rare breed! You are a treasure to be found and held dear by the people in your life.

When we look at the Hebrew word for *worthy* in this verse, we find that a worthy woman is *excellent, mighty, worthy, efficient, and valiant.*[2] This word is used 243 times in the Old Testament of the Bible, and more than half of those occurrences are in a military context, rich with armor and battle symbolism.

The word used to describe the Proverbs 31 woman is also written in the book of Judges to describe a mighty warrior! How amazing is that?

At the time of Judges, Israel had been oppressed for years by their enemy, Midian. Their hordes had struck terror in the hearts of God's people with constant raids upon their homes, livestock, and crops. No one had come forward to lead the Israelites against such a fierce enemy. When Israel cried out for help, God called an ordinary man named Gideon to step into leadership:

" *The angel of the Lord came and sat down under the oak in Ophrah that belonged to Joash the Abiezrite, where his son Gideon was threshing wheat in a winepress to keep it from the Midianites. When the angel of the Lord appeared to Gideon, he said, "The Lord is with you, **mighty warrior.**"*

"Pardon me, my lord," Gideon replied, "but if the Lord is with us, why has all this happened to us? Where are all his wonders that our ancestors told us about when they said, 'Did not the Lord

bring us up out of Egypt?' But now the Lord has abandoned us and given us into the hand of Midian."

The Lord turned to him and said, "Go in the strength you have and save Israel out of Midian's hand. Am I not sending you?"

"Pardon me, my lord," Gideon replied, "but how can I save Israel? My clan is the weakest in Manasseh, and I am the least in my family."

The Lord answered, "I will be with you, and you will strike down all the Midianites, leaving none alive." Judges 6:11-16

Notice that God called Gideon a "mighty warrior" when he was feeling weak and thinking he was the least of those around him. The Lord saw Gideon's potential and spoke about "the nonexistent things that He has foretold and promised *as if they already existed*" (Romans 4:17). This is something we are going to uncover repeatedly in Proverbs 31. I believe the Lord will speak words over you that are consistent with the vision and the plans that He has for you. You may not believe these things to be true about yourself…at least not yet! You will not be required to perform these things, only participate with Him as He affirms you, grows you, and transforms you.

If you finish the story of Gideon, you'll see that he takes some time to confirm what the Lord is asking of him, and then he steps out into battle, showing how virtuous and valiant he can be with the Spirit of God propelling him from within.

Daughter of God, you are valiant. You have a warrior's heart. You know when to fight for the one who has no voice. You know when to fight for truth and justice. You know when to speak up.

You are as valiant as Gideon, and you don't even know it. You have been a mighty warrior and you will be again every time the occasion calls for it. You will be valiant every time that God empowers you to fight and stand for the things that He calls you to.

✿ Are there ways or areas in which you already feel like a warrior?

✿ In what ways or areas do you need God's help to be a warrior?

✿ Talk with Him about the things that are waging war against you. Let Him strengthen you for what's to come. He is with you always.

Day 5: You Are Valuable

For her price is far above rubies. {Proverbs 31:10}

What a lovely comparison is found here in verse 10! You are more precious than jewels. Your value is far above precious stones such as rubies or pearls. Many women struggle with believing that they are valuable. We tend to think our value comes from how we look, what we can achieve, how much we are needed, or what we can contribute.

✺ Where do you (honestly) think your value comes from?

✺ What kinds of things do you find yourself doing to earn or prove your value?

The Sunrise Ruby, the most expensive ruby in the world to date, was given an estimated value of $12-18 million prior to being auctioned in May 2015. This 25-carat blood red ruby sold at auction for over $30 million.[3] Its value was established not only by size, color, clarity, and rarity but also by what someone was willing to pay for it.

The phrase we are looking at today in Proverbs 31:10 reads beautifully in The Passion Translation of the Bible (TPT). *"The price paid for her was greater than many jewels."* There is a footnote in the text for this verse that reads, "The price paid for her was the sacred blood of the Lamb of God, her Bridegroom." Like the Sunrise Ruby, our value is determined by what someone is willing to pay for us.

This is not a price worked out by what you bring to the table. It is not based on what you can accomplish or how fruitful you are. Nor is it affected by how obedient or self-controlled you are. It is a value measured by how much the Father loves you and cherishes you. Your worth is determined by the price He was willing to pay for you. You merit the ultimate sacrifice that the Father made when He gave His Son to die on the cross.

You are a precious treasure. You are the apple of God's eye (Deuteronomy 32:10). You were made by Him. You were redeemed by His Son. You have been called by God. You are precious in His sight.

" Do not fear, for I have redeemed you; I have summoned you by name; you are mine. When you pass through the waters, I will be with you; and when you pass through the rivers, they will not sweep over you. When you walk through the fire, you will not be burned; the flames will not set you ablaze. For I am the Lord your God, the Holy One of Israel, your Savior; I give Egypt for your ransom, Cush and Seba in your stead. **Since you are precious and honored in my sight, and because I love you**, *I will give people in exchange for you, nations in exchange for your life. Isaiah 43:1b-4*

✹ Read the previous verses again. What speaks to you the most?

✹ Write a response to the Lord's declaration of your worth. What do you want to say to Him?

Day 6: You Are Trustworthy

The heart of her husband trusts in her. {Proverbs 31:11}

This verse speaks about a married woman, but let's take a deeper look. The Scriptures use marriage as a metaphor for our relationship with the Lord in both the Old and the New Testaments. Here is a verse to ponder, addressed to God's people:

Your maker is your husband—the Lord of Hosts is His name.
Isaiah 54:5

✤ What comes to mind when you consider that the Lord is like a husband to you?

✤ Sit quietly for a moment and let the Holy Spirit speak a word to your heart. Record here any words, thoughts, responses.

Let us consider verse 11 of Proverbs 31 as though God is our husband. His heart trusts in you! Maybe you wrestle with the idea of God trusting you. It's an interesting thing to contemplate. As I began to question this idea and pray on it, the Lord reminded me that He has entrusted us with His very Presence-- the Holy Spirit living within every believer. He has endowed us with the gifts of the Spirit. He has entrusted us with the Gospel. He has assigned us to care for His people: family, friends, neighbors, disciples, co-workers, students, and more. Why would God do this if He did not trust us and believe in us?

" But you are a chosen people, a royal priesthood, a holy nation, God's special possession, that you may declare the praises of him who called you out of darkness into his wonderful light. 1 Peter 2:9

We must assume that He believes we are capable of managing the gifts, people, and resources that He has bestowed in our lives. Of course, we cannot manage these things on our own. We need the guidance, power, and transformation of the Holy Spirit. We need His word to show us the way.

You are chosen. You belong to God, who has called you into His marvelous light. You are being transformed and He can already see what you will become. He invests so much in you because He trusts you and believes in you.

§ Is there something that the Lord has entrusted to you that you struggle with? Pour your heart out to Him about this.

✹ Is there something that you long to have Him trust you with? Bring this before the Lord.

✹ Have any perspectives changed for you today?

Day 7: You Are a Worthwhile Investment

The heart of her husband trusts in her.
He shall have no lack of gain. {Proverbs 31:11}

A Proverbs 31 woman provides a gainful return when someone invests in her. This is beneficial in many relationships: friendship, marriage, mentorship, business partners, leadership, and more.

✿ Can you think of a person who has invested in your life? What kind of gain has come from that relationship?

✿ How about a person (or people) that you have poured into? What benefit has resulted?

The principle of investments and returns applies to our relationship with God as well. He has made the greatest investment of all in you—and it has been worth it. He receives a great return on what He pours into you. Every time that you respond to His call or submit to His guidance, He accomplishes

His purposes. In each moment that you trust Him in difficult situations, you and God both experience spiritual gain.

" *For as the rain and snow come down from heaven, and do not return to it without watering the earth and making it bud and flourish, so that it yields seed for the sower and bread for the eater, so is my word that goes out from my mouth: It will not return to me empty, but will accomplish what I desire and achieve the purpose for which I sent it.   Isaiah 55:10-11*

❀ How have God's words in the Bible produced a spiritual gain in your life? If you're not sure, ask the Lord to show you an example.

❀ Do you wrestle with truly feeling like "a worthwhile investment" to the Lord? Talk to Him about it.

Day 8: You Are a Vessel of Goodness

She does him good, and not harm, all the days of her life.
{Proverbs 31:12}

In all honesty, this verse is quite intimidating! Doing *good, and not harm* to others 100% of the time is something that only God is capable of, yet it's easy to internalize this verse as an expectation for ourselves to always do good.

I ran myself ragged for many years trying to achieve it. When I look back on it now, I see that my motives were more about trying to *be* good enough for God and others rather than trying to truly *bring* good into others' lives.

✿ Can you relate to this struggle? How so?

The Spirit of God in us brings good to others. His guidance shows us what others need. His Word stored up in our hearts brings encouragement to others. Our presence in the lives of others, infused with God's Presence, is a conduit of good. God can pour out His goodness to others *through us* when we make ourselves available.

" *For by grace you have been saved through faith, and that not of yourselves; it is the gift of God—not the result of works, lest anyone should boast. For we are His workmanship, created in*

Christ Jesus for good works, which God prepared beforehand that we should walk in them.   Ephesians 2:8-10 (NKJV)

Look at those verses again. Did you notice that God is the one who prepares our good works? We are called to walk in them, to step into them once God has initiated them and signaled us to go. Meditate and pray on that for a moment.

How many times have we decided what would be "good" in a situation, only to watch God do something completely different, bringing more blessing than you could have imagined? We must rely on God's sense of "good", not our own. Perfection is not required. Sometimes good is misinterpreted or carried out with wrong motives. It's okay to get it wrong sometimes. Just wait for the next cue to be a vessel of His goodness.

❀ How have you struggled with doing good?   Talk to the Lord about that struggle.

❀ Is there any good that He has prepared for you today? Ask Him to help you walk in what He has laid out.

Day 9: You Are Creative

She seeks wool and flax, and works eagerly with her willing hands. {Proverbs 31:13}

Here we see the cultural and industrial differences between the time that Proverbs was written and now. I don't know about you, but I haven't handled much wool and flax in their harvested form. Most of us do not have to worry about developing raw materials into thread and fabric for our clothing and household goods like the Proverbs 31 woman did.

However, God has placed raw materials in our lives that we are gifted and called to develop with His help. We are created in the image of our Creator, who is a Master Craftsman, an Artist, an Inventor, and an Initiator. You have His creator DNA!

❀ Can you see how you have been made in His Creator image? Write them down here. Ask the Holy Spirit to bring them to your mind if you can't think of anything.

God has placed the building blocks for some truly amazing things in your life. Take His hand and serve with Him. Let God initiate and create things through your hands and your heart. Walk with Him so you can see what He has planned. All that He asks is for willingness and cooperation.

There is so much in life that is beyond your control. In your daily life, you will find some sort of wool and flax to grasp, form, and produce. Perhaps they are the only things you can control… do what you can and leave the rest to God.

" Whatever you do, work at it with all your heart, as working for the Lord, not for human masters, since you know that you will receive an inheritance from the Lord as a reward. It is the Lord Christ you are serving. Colossians 3:23-24

❀ What are the "wool and flax" in your life— the raw materials, gifts, or opportunities that He has given you? It may or may not be things that you can hold in your hands, so think broadly! If you don't know the answer, take a few minutes to pray on it and ask the Holy Spirit to show you.

❀ Is the Lord calling you to take any creative steps today? Talk to Him about it.

Day 10: You Have Beautiful Feet

She is like the merchant ships. She brings her bread from afar.
{Proverbs 31:14}

What an interesting comparison. No one has ever likened me to a ship before! However, I do appreciate some food-related praise. I love to feed my people, whether it's family or friends, and I will bring "bread from afar" for them. As I grow older, I am finding balance in this area, knowing when to cook and when to order out for food, when to set out a buffet of leftovers for dinner, and when to declare a potluck for a gathering. I don't need to do it all, and perfection is not the goal.

Let's go deeper into this. As much as God loves our desire to cook for others, serve, celebrate and be hospitable, He loves it, even more, when we provide spiritual food to those around us.

" *Jesus said to them, "Very truly I tell you, it is not Moses who has given you the bread from heaven, but it is my Father who gives you the true bread from heaven. For the bread of God is the bread that comes down from heaven and gives life to the world."*

"Sir," they said, "always give us this bread."

Then Jesus declared, "I am the bread of life. Whoever comes to me will never go hungry, and whoever believes in me will never be thirsty.   John 6:32-35

God has placed you in a specific network of His children for a reason. Just as God supplied manna in the wilderness for His people (Exodus 16), He is using you, and those around you, to offer spiritual nourishment to each other. Be open to His leading as He puts words on your tongue to share with others. Be ready to call, send a text, or write a note with God's words of life. You are His manna dispenser in your family and social circles.

✤ Can you think of a time when someone in your life shared a bit of the Bread of Life with you?

✤ Are you in need of some spiritual bread today? Be still with God for a moment and allow Him to speak a word to you.

❝ *How beautiful on the mountains are the feet of those who bring good news, who proclaim peace, who bring good tidings, who proclaim salvation, who say to Zion, "Your God reigns!"* Isaiah 52:7

You, my sister, have beautiful feet. You bring good news and words of peace and salvation to those around you. When a friend or family member needs to be reminded, you let them know that our loving God reigns over their lives and their circumstances. According to Proverbs 25:11, a relevant word spoken at the right moment is as valuable as "*apples of gold in settings of silver*". A few words can mean so much.

✺ Where might your beautiful feet take you to offer a bit of the bread of life to someone today? Let the Lord lead and supply.

Day 11: You Will Rise in the Night Season

She rises also while it is yet night. She gives food to her household. {Proverbs 31:15}

Yesterday's theme of caring for and feeding others continues today. However, there is an emphasis on rising quite early in this verse. Don't worry—God knows that we are not all early risers by nature. Some of us are night owls!

In my younger years, I had to set my alarm a good 45 minutes ahead of schedule so that I could hit the snooze button five times. Then came a season in my life that offered me very little alone time, and I discovered that rising well before everyone else in the house was necessary for my sanity. I learned to love those early morning hours! My life has shifted once again, and I don't feel the need to get up as early anymore. It's been good for me to let go of the idea that a godly woman gets up by a certain time.

Let's look at the phrase, *"She rises also while it is yet night"* in a figurative manner for a moment. Consider how The Passion Translation presents it: *"Even in the night season she arises"*. Let that sink in. Read it again.

❦ Have you had "night seasons" in your life?

❦ How did God meet you in those seasons and help you to rise?

One of my darkest seasons came several months after the Lord showed me that He was going to use me to share His Word in a mighty way. Of course, I made assumptions about what this would look like. I thought the Lord had shown me specifically what would happen next in my life, but when circumstances turned in the opposite direction, I was devastated. How could I have been so wrong about what He showed me? The whole experience shook my faith because I couldn't trust myself to hear His voice or discern His will anymore. It made me question nearly every area of my life.

God was faithful to walk me through it. He sat with me when I couldn't find the words to pray and when I stared blankly at the pages of my Bible, wondering if I understood any of it. He rebuilt my faith and my trust in Him, one day at a time.

I emerged from the other side of that season with more spiritual intimacy with God than ever. My faith felt brand new and more authentic. I learned some incredibly valuable lessons about laying everything at His feet… including any promises or visions that He might give me for the future.

I see now that the night season was necessary. I hadn't been remotely ready for the ministry adventures He had planned for me, until after I emerged from the darkness.

" *Arise, Jerusalem! Let your light shine for all to see. For the glory of the Lord rises to shine on you. Darkness as black as night covers all the nations of the earth, but the glory of the Lord rises and appears over you. All nations will come to your light; mighty kings will come to see your radiance. Look and see, for everyone is coming home! Your sons are coming from distant lands; your little daughters will be carried home. Your eyes will shine, and your heart will thrill with joy,   Isaiah 60:1-5a (NLT)*

❧ Read the previous passage from Isaiah again and allow the Holy Spirit to speak to you personally. Record any insights here:

❧ Respond to Him, if you haven't already.

46

Day 12: You Deserve Help

*She gives food to her household, and portions for her servant
girls. {Proverbs 31:15}*

This part of verse 15 might contain the best-kept secret of the
Proverbs 31 woman! I didn't discover it until a few years ago when
I read the Amplified Version:

> *She rises also while it is still night*
> *And gives food to her household*
> *And assigns tasks to her maids.*

The original wording of the text seems to lean more toward
providing or delegating *work tasks* rather than food. The word
portion may very well mean their *share* of the household work.

While we've been busy believing that women are responsible
for taking care of everyone in their vicinity, perhaps God was
trying to communicate the importance of delegating. Hmmmmm.
Give that some thought.

✿ What is your immediate reaction to the thought of God-ordained
delegation?

✿ As you meditate on the idea, what might God be speaking to
you?

Several years ago, my mental health reached a breaking point— thanks to my unbalanced ideas about what was expected of me as a woman. I clearly remember sobbing in my bedroom on Christmas morning that year because I had neglected to order a charger for my son's gift from Santa. (Who knew that it didn't come with a charger?) I honestly believed I had ruined Christmas because I was so fixated on making the day special for each person. The first sign of failure on my part sent me over the edge.

My Christmas example might seem petty, and my response disproportionate—and it was! At the time, I was driven by perfection, performance, and shame. I was convinced that godly women are responsible for everyone around them. I thank God that my breaking point came soon after that Christmas, and I began a quest to uncover and replace the performance and shame-based core beliefs I had about myself and my role as a woman.

I am here to say, "DELEGATE!' Talk to the people in your home about sharing the load. I was so bad at delegating that I would take offense if someone asked to help me. My brain interpreted offers for assistance as a sign that I wasn't measuring up. Crazy, right? Or maybe it doesn't seem irrational to you, because you've had similar thoughts.

Even after making my decision to start accepting help, I would fumble when people offered to assist. I honestly didn't know what to say sometimes, because I was still feeling inadequate for needing support. I started to use "you can help with the dishes, thank you," as my automatic response when someone asked to help in my home, but I didn't know what to say. Baby steps!

Sister, you can delegate at home, at work, and church. It's often as simple as *actually taking the help that has been offered to you for years!* Let coworkers use their talents to support you. Let people bring food to events that you host at home or church. Let a friend or relative come early to help you set up. Let people stay after to help clean up. Use pretty paper goods on holidays to cut down on dishes and bribe the kids in your life to do extra chores in preparation and clean up. They love you and they want to help you.

" *"Each of you should use whatever gift you have received **to serve others**, as faithful stewards of God's grace in its various forms. 1 Peter 4:10*

We may understand the general meaning of this verse penned by Peter, but we miss the secondary meaning. Take another look at the words above. God placed people in your life to use their gifts to serve YOU as faithful extenders of His grace. Let them! Don't steal their joy or their opportunity to serve God by assisting you.

✿ What beliefs about being a godly woman have served to harm you rather than motivate you?

✿ Are there any habits or beliefs God is prompting you to lay aside?

✺ Sit quietly for a moment and let God speak to you about His plans and expectations for you as a woman. Record any insights here.

Day 13: Your Territory Will Expand

She considers a field and buys it. {Proverbs 31:16}

Here we see the Proverbs 31 woman carefully considering an investment to increase the family's assets. While many of us may not have the chance to invest in undeveloped land, we do have opportunities to develop our careers, ministries, families, finances, or circles of influence. It can be difficult at times to make decisions about broadening areas of our lives because we aren't fully assured that the risk will pay off. However, God can see the future! That is why it's so important to let God enlarge our lives instead of trying to do it on our own.

✿ Have you ever tried to expand something on your own? How did it turn out?

More often than not, God desires to widen our perspective and our understanding of His ways *before* He enlarges our territory. He often signals to us ahead of time that He is going to open a door of expansion for us. Naturally, we get excited and start making preparations. We might set up timelines in our minds, then find ourselves experiencing frustrating delays. This is due to the unfinished inner development God wants to do *first*. We must not lose hope, or give up on His promise to expand our territory! Slow down and tune in to the inner work of growth and transformation the Lord wants to do first.

Spiritual growth consistently comes from experiencing a deeper understanding of the love of God. We know in our minds that we are loved unconditionally, but we forget that His love has unfathomable depths. The path to experiencing the fullness of God is comprehending these depths, one layer at a time.

" I pray that out of his glorious riches he may strengthen you with power through his Spirit in your inner being, so that Christ may dwell in your hearts through faith. And I pray that you, being rooted and established in love, may have power, together with all the Lord's holy people, to grasp how wide and long and high and deep is the love of Christ, and to know this love that surpasses knowledge—that you may be filled to the measure of all the fullness of God. Ephesians 3:16-19

A revelation of God's love for you personally will do wonders for your faith and your journey. When you can conceive how fully and completely His love embraces you, chases you, catches you when you fall, and carries you, then you are more prepared to step into the newly expanded world He has opened to you.

" For I am convinced that neither death nor life, neither angels nor demons, neither the present nor the future, nor any powers, neither height nor depth, nor anything else in all creation, will be able to separate us from the love of God in Christ Jesus our Lord. Romans 8:38-39

❀ Perhaps you are waiting for some kind of enlargement. Can you tell what God is doing to prepare you for it?

✺ How can you more fully participate in this preparation?

✺ Ask Him for a deeper revelation of His love for you (consider making this a regular prayer!). Sit and wait for a word, an image, or a verse from Him.

Day 14: You Are Fruitful

With the fruit of her hands, she plants a vineyard.
{Proverbs 31:16}

For many years, I was under the impression that fruitfulness came from my devotion and hard work: plant the seeds, water them, toil over everything, and make the fruit grow while the Lord watches over everything. However, fruitfulness comes from the Holy Spirit's work within us and the hand of God moving around us. Honestly, the key to our fruitfulness is less about *doing* and more about *being connected.* Consider Jesus' words on the subject:

❝ *Remain in me, as I also remain in you. No branch can bear fruit by itself; it must remain in the vine. Neither can you bear fruit unless you remain in me. I am the vine; you are the branches. If you remain in me and I in you, you will bear much fruit; apart from me you can do nothing. If you do not remain in me, you are like a branch that is thrown away and withers. John 15:4-6a*

✿ Read that passage again. What stood out to you? What might the Holy Spirit be communicating to you?

Fruitfulness is directly linked to our dependence and trust. The more we trust and depend on God, the more fruit His Holy Spirit can bear in us and around us. We participate in the fruit-bearing, but it is not our sole responsibility! It's easy to be a branch running amok, trying to produce fruit on our own. We may not realize how much we have disconnected from the vine until we feel very withered and dried up. The pressure and the failure become too much. Performing without connection with Him causes us to burn out.

✤ Have you worn yourself out trying to be fruitful? How so? Talk to the Lord about this.

✤ Are you sensing that the Holy Spirit wants to produce any particular fruit in you? Jot down any insight He may give you.

We are called to remain in Him, to abide or rest in His presence. We must allow Him to fill us and guide us. Think about a baby abiding in the womb of its mother. The babe is enveloped, nourished, and carried about. A child's most extraordinary period of growth happens while it is powerless to achieve any of its own transformation.

Beware of thinking that it is your job to bear fruit to please God. Let go of believing that you must transform yourself to be what He has called you to be. Rest in Him like a babe resting in the womb and let His Spirit bring growth and fruit.

✸ Close your eyes and ask the Lord to show you what resting in Him looks like. Record any insights here.

Day 15: You Are Strong

She arms her waist with strength, and makes her arms strong.
{Proverbs 31:17}

❦ Who do you admire as a strong woman?

❦ What qualities or abilities come to mind when you think of strength in a person?

Strong has been defined as "having the power to move heavy weights or perform other physically demanding tasks; able to withstand great force or pressure; not easily disturbed, upset, or affected; firmly held or established."[4]

❦ What thoughts or feelings does the definition above evoke for you?

Perhaps we look at Proverbs 31:17 and focus too quickly on the word *strength*, bypassing the word *arms* (or *girds* in some translations). She arms herself with strength, which means that she puts strength on like a weapon. Hold on to that for a minute. She does not summon strength from within, but gets it from somewhere and puts it on.

*" But we have this treasure in jars of clay to show that **this all-surpassing power is from God and not from us.** We are hard-pressed on every side, but not crushed; perplexed, but not in despair; persecuted, but not abandoned; struck down, but not destroyed.   2 Corinthians 4:7-9*

❀ What are you feeling today? Use one of the phrases from the verses in 2 Corinthians above, or write in your own words.

I am _____, but not _____.

Notice in these verses is that the writer does not pretend or put on airs about his life as a follower of Jesus. He knows he's hard-pressed, perplexed, persecuted, and struck down. He also knows WHERE his strength comes from. He doesn't play the part of a church leader who has it all together. Something about our Christian society presses us to believe we must have it all together. None of us do!

Have you ever been around a toddler that wanted to do something on her own? My firstborn's mantra at age three was, "I do it myself!" (Spoken at full volume). She would spend all of her energy and her will, trying to get it done before relenting and letting me help her. How often are we like that with the Lord? Sometimes we want to do things in our own strength to please

Him, or to prove that we can do it, and we often wait until we are exhausted from the effort before we ask for His help.

Maybe we are mistaken and believe that the Lord will hold our weakness against us. However, the opposite is true:

" *But he said to me, "My grace is sufficient for you, for my power is made perfect in weakness." Therefore I will boast all the more gladly about my weaknesses, so that Christ's power may rest on me. That is why, for Christ's sake, I delight in weaknesses, in insults, in hardships, in persecutions, in difficulties. For when I am weak, then I am strong. 2 Corinthians 12:9-10*

Here we are encouraged to embrace our weaknesses! In fact, weakness is a gateway to His strength. The sooner we recognize our weakness, our brokenness, and our emptiness, the sooner we can be filled with His strength.

The trouble is that we often despise our weaknesses. We look critically at them, instead of coming to terms with them. The irony is that your brokenness qualifies you to be filled, healed, strengthened, lifted up, and carried.

✺ Have you despised or embraced your brokenness?

✺ Talk to Jesus about all of this. Write down any encouragement that He gives you here.

Day 16: Your Work Is Good

She perceives that her merchandise is profitable. {Proverbs 31:18}

Various Bible translations of this verse state that she *perceives*, *senses*, or *sees* that her *profits*, *dealings*, or *merchandise* is good and profitable. Interestingly, the word used for *perceives* literally means *to taste*.[5] That implies that she knows firsthand that the work she does is valuable.

You are encouraged to taste and see that what you have accomplished by the will and power of the Lord is good and profitable. Do not allow others, or the world, to tell you that the work you have invested in is not good enough.

We live in a world that is inserting its views and opinions into our lives around the clock. Television, radio, social media, ads, magazines, emails, text messages, and more serve as input every waking hour of the day, and it is affecting our hearts, minds, and perspectives. I find that the amount of social media surfing that I do is directly proportional to my levels of peace and joy! Seeing too much of what the world thinks and does increases my expectations and decreases my satisfaction.

I read a quote on social media recently (Oh, the irony!) that said, "No one else is supposed to understand your calling, it wasn't a conference call."[6] This idea has lingered with me. Only God and I were present when He gave me glimpses of how He wanted to use my life to impact my family, my friends, my church, and the world. I don't need a person to affirm that calling or agree with it. I do need people in my life who support me in my calling, but they weren't there when God spoke. I have to stand on what He has shown me and where He is leading me. As I continue to write this book, it's easy to get worried that people will not agree with what I believe God has shown me about the Proverbs 31 woman. Nevertheless, I must keep writing and sharing. I can't worry about the people who won't understand my calling.

" Therefore, I urge you, brothers and sisters, in view of God's mercy, to offer your bodies as a living sacrifice, holy and pleasing to God—this is your true and proper worship. Do not conform to the pattern of this world, but be transformed by the renewing of your mind. Then you will be able to test and approve what God's will is—his good, pleasing and perfect will. Romans 12:1-2

Part of renewing our minds involves letting go of what the world has thrown at us and standing in the truth of who God is and who we are in His sight. When our minds are renewed, we are in a better position to "test and approve" God's will for our individual lives.

🌀 What has God whispered to you through the Bible and nudges of His Holy Spirit about your calling?

🌀 What concerns or fears do you have about your calling? Talk about them with the Lord.

Day 17: You Are Full of Light

Her lamp doesn't go out by night. {Proverbs 31:18}

When I first read this verse many years ago, I read it as an expectation to stay up until everything was done before I went to bed. This idea fell in line with the underlying drive I had to prove my value by doing everything perfectly and making everyone happy. Paired with the expectation I perceived in verse 15 to rise early each morning, I was a hot, sleep-deprived mess. Now that I am out from under those core beliefs of perfectionism and shame, I recognize that we are wired to be morning people *or* night owls, and should not try to do both. We need sleep and rest to function at our best.

Perhaps this verse is less about burning the midnight oil, and more about how women bring light into their circles of influence! I was surprised to learn that the word *lamp* that is used here is the same Hebrew word used in Exodus for the lampstand that provided light in the tabernacle and later in the temple.

❝ *"Make a lampstand of pure gold. Hammer out its base and shaft, and make its flowerlike cups, buds, and blossoms of one piece with them. Six branches are to extend from the sides of the lampstand—three on one side and three on the other. Three cups shaped like almond flowers with buds and blossoms are to be on one branch, three on the next branch, and the same for all six branches extending from the lampstand. Exodus 25: 31-33*

❝ *"Command the Israelites to bring you clear oil of pressed olives for the light so that the lamps may be kept burning. In the tent of meeting, outside the curtain that shields the ark of the covenant law, Aaron and his sons are to keep the lamps burning before the*

Lord from evening till morning. This is to be a lasting ordinance among the Israelites for the generations to come. Exodus 27: 20-21

The lamp in the tabernacle was especially important because there were no windows in the structure. The light from this lamp was a necessity. It was delicately designed with small cups that would hold oil and a fabric wick, where the flames would burn. The priests were commanded to keep the light burning all the time. In the morning and evening, they would fill the cups with oil and replace wicks if needed. Jewish tradition in the Talmud holds that even if the nighttime supply of oil was not enough to burn through to the morning, there would always be one flame that miraculously still burned.[7] It would appear that God kept the flame alive.

As light-bearers, we are not the source of light. The source is the oil of the Holy Spirit, who radiates the light of the Father. As long as we are filled with His Spirit and His light, it shines through us and offers light to those around us. Even when we are feeling empty and poured out, the Spirit of God ensures that we still have a flame burning within. He won't let it burn out. He won't let the enemy snuff it out.

❧ How has God used you to bring light to the people in your life? If you are unsure, ask the Lord to bring forth a memory of a time or situation where you shined His light.

✺ Do you feel assured that His light is shining through you? Talk to Him about any concerns you have.

✺ Imagine the lovely golden cups of the tabernacle lampstand being filled with oil and then lit to emanate light. Allow Him to fill you to overflowing as you rest in His presence.

Day 18: Your Mess is His Masterpiece

She lays her hands to the distaff, and her hands hold the spindle.
{Proverbs 31:19}

This verse may require a Google search! Few women today even know what a spindle and distaff are. (If you're a visual person, then an image search online might be helpful.) A spindle and distaff are a set of tools used in turning raw fibers into usable thread or yarn. The crude unspun flax or wool shreds are wrapped around the distaff and resemble a giant Q-tip. The user pulls at the fibers on the distaff and thins them out by twisting them into yarn or thread. The spindle is a wooden spike around which the thinned-out product is wrapped.[8] The Proverbs 31 woman used these tools to produce thread and yarn that she used to make all kinds of clothing and household items.

✺ What can we take away from this verse? Any initial thoughts?

I spent some time seeking the Lord and even recruited some prayer friends to join me, as I waited for the Lord to show me if there was a deeper meaning here. He whispered to my heart:

The distaff and spindle illustrate how I lay hold of the raw and tangled mess of your life and smooth it out. I take the unspun chaos and make it useful for both the practical and the beautiful. Just as rough, twisted fibers of flax and wool become everyday towels, diapers, and work clothes, they also become festive gowns, tablecloths, and colorful tapestries. The rough and knotted things in your life are smoothed out and transformed into victories, testimonies, and increased faith. Your mess is My masterpiece.

❀ How has the Lord done this in your life?

Only God can take the wounds and failures of our lives and make them into something beautiful and glorious. Only He can take the hardest and ugliest things in our lives and end up bringing good out of them. You can trust Him with the tangled mess of your life. Nothing is too twisted. Nothing is beyond His ability to redeem.

" *I consider that our present sufferings are not worth comparing with the glory that will be revealed in us. For the creation waits in eager expectation for the children of God to be revealed. For the creation was subjected to frustration, not by its own choice, but by the will of the one who subjected it, in hope that the creation itself will be liberated from its bondage to decay and brought into the freedom and glory of the children of God. Romans 8:18-21*

" *And we know that in all things God works for the good of those who love him, who have been called according to his purpose. For those God foreknew he also predestined to be conformed to the image of his Son, that he might be the firstborn among many brothers and sisters. And those he predestined, he also called; those he called, he also justified; those he justified, he also glorified. Romans 8:28-30*

✾ What stood out to you the most in the previous verses?

Daughter of our Heavenly Father, because you are made in His image, you too can smooth out tangled messes between loved ones, friends, children, and coworkers. God has used you to untangle misunderstandings and snap judgments. This is one of the many ways He has created you in His image. So lay hold of the metaphorical distaff and spindle when He calls you to smooth out some rough edges. Allow Him to dispense His grace and patience with the people in your lives that need a peacemaker, an advocate, or a referee. Do not put pressure on yourself to make everyone get along. Just be available when God nudges you to step in.

✾ How has the Lord spoken to you today?

Day 19: You Are a Blessing to Others

She opens her arms to the poor;
Yes, she extends her hands to the needy.
{Proverbs 31:20}

At first glance, the Proverbs writer seems to repeat the same idea twice in a row here. However, when we look closely at the subtle differences, a rich double meaning is revealed.

The Proverbs 31 woman spreads out her arms in a welcoming, receiving way. She also reaches forth, extending help to those who may not want to ask. She opens physical arms filled with provision, but she also extends a figurative hand symbolizing her influence and connections. She cares not only about the financially poor, but also the oppressed, the weak, the emotionally and relationally poor, the spiritually poor, and the humble, who won't ask.

Let's be clear that women are not required to do ALL of these things. Recognize how much you've already done, and can do, by broadening the definition of poor and needy.

Even if we are not able to give much financially, we can give emotionally, relationally, or spiritually. We will encounter many people whose greatest needs have little to do with finances.

Also, remember that wealth is relative! Consider my middle-class American family, which would seem deprived by Beverly Hills' standards, but extremely rich by the standards of third world nations. We have had seasons of life when we felt poor, and God used others to extend provision to us. More often, we've had seasons when we were in the position to bless others that were in need.

Not only is wealth relative, but so is the value of our charity to others. What seems like a small thing for you to give, might be a substantial thing for someone else to receive.

" *Jesus sat down opposite the place where the offerings were put and watched the crowd putting their money into the temple treasury. Many rich people threw in large amounts. But a poor widow came and put in two very small copper coins, worth only a few cents.*

Calling his disciples to him, Jesus said, "Truly I tell you, this poor widow has put more into the treasury than all the others. They all gave out of their wealth; but she, out of her poverty, put in everything—all she had to live on." Mark 12:41-44

❀ How have you been blessed by the generosity and compassion of someone else in your time of need?

❀ How has God used you to meet the needs of someone who was physically, emotionally, spiritually, or relationally poor?

✺ Is God bringing anyone in particular to your mind right now? Ask the Lord to show you how you can bless them.

Day 20: Time for Reflection

We are halfway through the Proverbs 31 passage! Let's take some time to review what we've read so far.

> " *Who can find a worthy woman?*
> *For her price is far above rubies.*
> *The heart of her husband trusts in her.*
> *He shall have no lack of gain.*
> *She does him good, not harm, all the days of her life.*
> *She seeks wool and flax, and works eagerly with her hands.*
> *She is like the merchant ships.*
> *She brings her bread from afar.*
> *She rises also while it is yet night, gives food to her household, and portions for her servant girls.*
> *She considers a field and buys it.*
> *With the fruit of her hands, she plants a vineyard.*
> *She arms her waist with strength, and makes her arms strong.*
> *She perceives that her merchandise is profitable.*
> *Her lamp doesn't go out by night.*
> *She lays her hands to the distaff, and her hands hold the spindle.*
> *She opens her arms to the poor; yes, she extends her hands to the needy.*
> *She is not afraid of the snow for her household; for all her household are clothed with scarlet.*
> *She makes for herself carpets of tapestry.*
> *Her clothing is fine linen and purple.*
> *Her husband is respected in the gates, when he sits among the elders of the land.*

She makes linen garments and sells them, and delivers sashes to the merchant.
Strength and dignity are her clothing.
She laughs at the time to come.
She opens her mouth with wisdom.
Kind instruction is on her tongue.
She looks well to the ways of her household, and doesn't eat the bread of idleness.
Her children rise up and call her blessed.
Her husband also praises her: "Many women do noble things, but you excel them all."
Charm is deceitful, and beauty is vain; but a woman who fears Yahweh, she shall be praised.
Give her of the fruit of her hands!
Let her works praise her in the gates!
Proverbs 31:10-31

❀ Have you discovered any unhelpful views that you once held of the Proverbs 31 woman?

❀ What new insights have been helpful?

❧ In what ways have you felt affirmed by God as you read through Proverbs 31 with new eyes?

❧ Do you sense some new work that the Lord is doing in you? Talk to Him about it.

Day 21: You Will Endure the Winter

She is not afraid of the snow for her household,
for all her household are clothed with scarlet.
{Proverbs 31:21}

The Proverbs 31 woman is not worried about the winter because she has prepared for what's to come. Depending on where you live, you may have a considerable amount of preparation to complete before snow and ice arrives, or you may only need to do a little shopping for seasonal clothes.

Preparation is one of those hands-on things we get to do that often gives us a sense of control over a coming change or transition. However, once everything has been gathered and put in order, we must shift into a different mode. There isn't anything to do except wait for the season to arrive and trust that all is ready. Preparation is necessary, but it's no guarantee that everything will go as expected.

In our lives, we will face more than one kind of winter. Some periods of our lives feel cold, or isolated, and our pathways may seem impossible to clear. We may feel like the days are short and the nights are long. Perhaps we might feel "snowed in"... trapped in a particular place or situation.

✿ Have you ever experienced a season that felt like winter?

The only thing that might be harder than enduring a winter season is watching a loved one go through it and not being able to stop it. That kind of powerlessness can be debilitating! Loving others can make us feel like we are responsible for them and their well-being. Loving others can hurt so deeply when we are faced with the fact that we have very little command over worrisome circumstances.

In truth, we have power over almost nothing in our lives. I've narrowed it down to just a few areas that are within control: our own attitudes, words, and actions. We can't rule others, their reactions, their choices, or their desires. We can't make our loved ones safe from everything. We can't make them want anything in particular, even if it's good for them. We can't fix the outcomes of their attitudes, words, or actions. We can't control what others do to our loved ones.

Once upon a time, I thought I could command all of the things above. I was a jumble of fear, anxiety, worrying and control, running scenarios and trying to say just the right words to make things go my way. I was so very unhappy all of the time.

God took me on a journey of letting go of (my illusion of) control. He taught me to lean into the powerlessness of my life and trust Him with all of the people and the outcomes. Oh, I still struggle sometimes, but when those feelings of fear and anxiety come, I recognize them for what they are: *a sign that I am feeling powerless over something very important to me*.

When the anxiety comes, it is time for us to take a deep breath, drawing air through the nose and slowly out through the mouth. We confess our trust in the Lord, repeatedly. It can take many repetitions before we truly mean it. We work at laying down the desire for control and visualize releasing the person or problem to Jesus.

Permit me to share Matthew 16:24-26 with some emphasis that spoke to me regarding control. Of course, this isn't the traditional way to interpret the verses, but it is quite powerful:

" Then Jesus said to his disciples, "Whoever wants to be my disciple must deny themselves {control} and take up their cross and follow me. For whoever wants to {control} their life will lose it, but whoever {surrenders} their life for me will find it. What good will it be for someone to gain {control of} the whole world, yet forfeit their soul? Or what can anyone give in exchange for their soul?

The Proverbs 31 woman does not fear the winter seasons that come for herself or her loved ones. She makes all of her preparations and then leans into the powerlessness of this life, putting her full trust in Jesus to provide through the winter and usher in the spring when it is time.

✺ What is the Lord whispering to you today?

✺ What is your response to Him?

Day 22: Your Needs Matter

She makes for herself carpets of tapestry. {Proverbs 31:22}

At first glance, today's verse speaks to creativity, home decor, and do-it-yourself projects. A woman's ability to create a welcoming environment shows here. While wrestling all of these ideas out in my mind, a few of the words suddenly jumped out at me: She makes *for herself*...!

Let that settle in for a moment. Nearly everything we've read so far is about what the Proverbs 31 woman does for others, and now we see that she does something for herself.

✺ What is something that you do for yourself that brings you joy or rest, or a boost to your vitality?

✺ Is there something that you want to start doing for yourself?

You might be familiar with the phrase "love your neighbor as yourself". It's used nine times in the Bible, especially by Jesus.

❝ One of the teachers of the law came and heard them debating. Noticing that Jesus had given them a good answer, he asked him, "Of all the commandments, which is the most important?"

83

"The most important one," answered Jesus, "is this: 'Hear, O Israel: The Lord our God, the Lord is one. Love the Lord your God with all your heart and with all your soul and with all your mind and with all your strength.' The second is this: 'Love your neighbor as yourself.' There is no commandment greater than these." Mark 12:28-31

Loving your neighbor as you would love yourself is a great thing to aspire to. The principle here is that we should treat others the way we want to be treated. The trouble with this line of teaching is that many of us, as women, treat others so much better than we treat ourselves.

❀ When the Proverbs 31 woman does something "for herself", perhaps she is working to love herself as well as she loves others. How does this resonate with you?

❀ If He hasn't already, ask the Lord to show you how you can take better care of yourself. Record any insights here.

❀ Make a plan to do something for yourself this week. Write it down below and also in your calendar!

Day 23: You Are Robed in Righteousness

Her clothing is fine linen and purple. {Proverbs 31:22}

The clothing of the Proverbs 31 woman clearly shows her wealth and status in the community. The fine linen material was the finest that could be found, similar to what is used to make the garments worn by priests in the Temple.[9] I can't help but wonder if she worried as much about her appearance as most women do today.

We spend so much time and energy trying to make our bodies the right size and shape. We feel pressure to dress as well as those around us. Billions of dollars are spent each year targeted toward women who want to appear thinner and younger. We are bombarded with messages all day long that undermine our confidence in the body that God gave us. Society seems to honor the wisdom of the aged, but not the physical progression that naturally comes with it.

Jesus had something to say about clothing and food. He doesn't want us worrying about cooking and eating all the "right" foods. He doesn't want us feeling anxious about how we are dressed or what size we are. You've likely read the following passage many times, but when you read it now, consider that it may relate to what we are discussing today.

❝ Therefore I tell you, do not worry about your life, what you will eat or drink; or about your body, what you will wear. Is not life more than food, and the body more than clothes? Look at the birds of the air; they do not sow or reap or store away in barns, and yet your heavenly Father feeds them. Are you not much more valuable than they? Can any one of you by worrying add a single hour to your life?

"And why do you worry about clothes? See how the flowers of the field grow. They do not labor or spin. Yet I tell you that not even Solomon in all his splendor was dressed like one of these. If that is how God clothes the grass of the field, which is here today and tomorrow is thrown into the fire, will he not much more clothe you—you of little faith? So do not worry, saying, 'What shall we eat?' or 'What shall we drink?' or 'What shall we wear?' For the pagans run after all these things, and your heavenly Father knows that you need them. But seek first his kingdom and his righteousness, and all these things will be given to you as well. Matthew 6:25-33

🌀 What are your thoughts as you read this in a new light?

Let us remember that, in the spiritual realm, the Lord has already dressed us even more splendidly than the Proverbs 31 woman.

" *I delight greatly in the Lord; my soul rejoices in my God. For he has clothed me with garments of salvation and arrayed me in a robe of his righteousness, as a bridegroom adorns his head like a priest, and as a bride adorns herself with her jewels. Isaiah 61:10*

🌀 Close your eyes and imagine Jesus offering you His robe of righteousness and then draping it on your shoulders. What thoughts or feelings come?

Remember that we do not receive His righteousness because we deserve it, or because of anything we have done. God chooses to showcase His glory, His love, His power, and His righteousness in us, broken vessels that He can shine through.

" *Brothers and sisters, think of what you were when you were called. Not many of you were wise by human standards; not many were influential; not many were of noble birth. But God chose the foolish things of the world to shame the wise; God chose the weak things of the world to shame the strong. God chose the lowly things of this world and the despised things—and the things that are not—to nullify the things that are, so that no one may boast before him. It is because of him that you are in Christ Jesus, who has become for us wisdom from God—that is, our righteousness, holiness and redemption. 1 Corinthians 1:26-30*

❀ Is there anything you've been wearing instead of His robes? If you are not sure, ask the Lord to show you. Write down anything that the Spirit brings to your mind.

❀ Talk to the Lord about what He has shown you today.

Day 24: You Were Made for Leadership

Her husband is respected in the gates,
when he sits among the elders of the land.
{Proverbs 31:23}

Today's verse is a great example of why we should not take Proverbs 31 too literally and allow it to establish unrealistic expectations in our lives. How can the passage be a specific mandate for all women, when God has not called every woman into marriage?

Of course, we don't want to dismiss this part completely, so I asked the Lord to put it into perspective. What does verse 23 mean for all of us... married, single, widowed, young, old, whether in public service or living a quiet private life?

God drew my attention to the concept of leadership. The Proverbs 31 woman and her husband were both known and respected as leaders in their community. This is an important part of the believer's life—to be the hands and feet of Jesus and shine His light wherever one goes. Whether on a large scale or small, you and I are called to lead somewhere. Perhaps you are leading children at home, in church, or at school. Maybe you are shepherding many, or maybe you are leading only one person! You may lead in the workplace, in your neighborhood, at church, in the community, online, or among your friends.

" *For by the grace given me I say to every one of you: Do not think of yourself more highly than you ought, but rather think of yourself with sober judgment, in accordance with the faith God has distributed to each of you. For just as each of us has one body with many members, and these members do not all have the same function, so in Christ we, though many, form one body, and* *each member belongs to all the others. We have different gifts, according to the grace given to each of us. If your gift is prophesying, then prophesy in accordance with your faith; if it is serving, then serve; if it is teaching, then teach; if it is to encourage, then give encouragement; if it is giving, then give generously; if it is to lead, do it diligently; if it is to show mercy, do it cheerfully. Romans 12:3-8*

Hasn't God done marvelous work in you? There are gifts, experience, wisdom, insight, and hope that you can offer to others. You may feel as though you are many steps behind most of the people in your life, but you are still ahead of others. That is what leadership is about! It is offering a hand to the person who is walking a path similar to one that you have already traveled. The relationship doesn't have to be exclusively spiritual; the opportunity to address spiritual things usually comes in time.

Leadership results in what I call "the fishbowl life". When we lead in any arena, we invite the people that we lead to view our lives up close and personally, as though we were living in a fishbowl on their kitchen counter. The Proverbs 31 woman knew what it was like to live this life. Was she perfect? It might seem so, but the answer is no! She wasn't perfect. Her children, her neighbors, folks in the marketplace, and at the Temple watched her living life each day. They saw her challenges, her victories, and some of her failures. They saw her apologize, pick herself up after a fall, and learn from her mistakes.

Living in the leadership fishbowl can bring about many temptations: to perform, to hide imperfections, to cover up failures, to keep up with others, to wear a mask, to generate fake personas. Daughter, do not give in to these temptations. Do not work to impress the spectators. You have only One Person to please, and you do that most successfully by being your genuine, transformed self.

When I think about the people in my life that I have the most respect for, they are people who have allowed me to see some of their weaknesses or failures. What a gift to see the grace of God and the transformational power of the Holy Spirit at work in their lives! People who live a (seemingly) perfect life leave me with the expectation to do the same. I'd rather share life with a broken and transformed person than one who appears to have it all together.

When in doubt, the best way to lead is Jesus' way. He led by serving. He led with the authority given Him, but always deferred to the Father in humility. He led in everyday settings, talking about everyday things as they related to the Kingdom of God. He was approachable and available but made time to recharge alone.

❝ *"You call me 'Teacher' and 'Lord,' and rightly so, for that is what I am. Now that I, your Lord and Teacher, have washed your feet, you also should wash one another's feet. I have set you an example that you should do as I have done for you. Very truly I tell you, no servant is greater than his master, nor is a messenger greater than the one who sent him. Now that you know these things, you will be blessed if you do them. John 13:13-17*

✿ What do you find difficult when it comes to leadership?

✿ Bring this difficulty to the Lord and ask for His insight.

✿ Could God be preparing you for a new leadership venture? Talk to Him about this.

Day 25: You Are Gifted

She makes linen garments and sells them;
and delivers sashes to the merchant.
{Proverbs 31:24}

Remember on day 9 when we read about taking raw materials (the wool and flax of our lives) and developing them with the Lord's help? Today, we are looking at the results of the Proverbs 31 woman's labor. She made something beautiful and practical out of wool and flax. We are all gifted in different ways by the Creator and blessed with gifts of the Holy Spirit. Some people might think that creative gifts are of no use to God or the body of believers, but Scripture says otherwise. Consider all of the creative skills required to make the Tabernacle:

" Every skilled woman spun with her hands and brought what she had spun—blue, purple or scarlet yarn or fine linen. And all the women who were willing and had the skill spun the goat hair. Then Moses said to the Israelites, "See, the Lord has chosen Bezalel son of Uri, the son of Hur, of the tribe of Judah, and he has filled him with the Spirit of God, with wisdom, with understanding, with knowledge and with all kinds of skills— to make artistic designs for work in gold, silver and bronze, to cut and set stones, to work in wood and to engage in all kinds of artistic crafts. And he has given both him and Oholiab son of Ahisamak, of the tribe of Dan, the ability to teach others. He has filled them with skill to do all kinds of work as engravers, designers, embroiderers in blue, purple and scarlet yarn and fine linen, and weavers—all of them skilled workers and designers. Exodus 35:25-26,30-35

God used ordinary people who had creative gifts to assemble the place where He would meet with His people. What a privilege to make something so special! Seamstresses, weavers, woodworkers, welders, jewelers, engravers, embroiderers, artists, and more were needed. God also required visionaries, surveyors, schedulers, planners, accountants, inventory keepers, communicators, assistants, problem solvers, foremen, and clean-up crews. No gift is useless in God's Kingdom.

❀ Did anything in the verses above surprise you or challenge your current beliefs about what kinds of gifts can be used to honor the Lord?

❀ What kinds of gifts do you possess (creative or otherwise)?

❀ Press in and ask the Lord to show you how you can use your gifts, or give you confirmation that you are already doing so.

Day 26: Like Father, Like Daughter

Strength and dignity are her clothing. {Proverbs 31:25}

On day 15, we discussed strength and how it is *not* something that comes from within, but something the Proverbs 31 woman receives from God and puts on. Today's verse reinforces that idea with the visual image of wearing strength and dignity as clothing.

Dignity is a word that we often have difficulty defining clearly. We talk in society today about *human dignity* as a right to be respected and treated in an ethical way as a person. However, dignity is technically not a right, but "a quality of being worthy of honor or respect".[10] Interestingly, the word *dignity* used in verse 25 is usually translated from Hebrew to English as *glory, honor, or majesty.* What an interesting word to use for women!

You might be surprised to learn that the same two attributes given to the Proverbs 31 woman in today's verse (strength and dignity/majesty) are also used for God in Psalm 96.

" *For great is the Lord and most worthy of praise; He is to be feared above all gods. For all the gods of the nations are idols, but the Lord made the heavens. Splendor and* **majesty** *are before him;* **strength** *and glory are in his sanctuary.   Psalm 96:4-6*

Quite simply, the phrase "like father, like daughter" applies here. You were made in the majestic and strong image of your Father. The exact Hebrew words are used to describe both you and God. If you're not convinced, take the next few verses in:

*" When I consider your heavens, the work of your fingers, the moon, and the stars, which you have set in place, what is mankind that you are mindful of them, human beings that you care for them? You have made them a little lower than the angels and crowned them with glory and **honor**.   Psalm 8:3-5*

The Proverbs 31 woman is not clothed with strength and dignity because she executes these qualities on her own. She is clothed and crowned by her Father in Heaven, who has made her in His image. You are clothed with majesty and strength and honor because you are a beloved daughter of the Most High God.

❀ How does it feel knowing that our Proverbs 31 verse uses words to describe women that are usually used to describe God?

❀ Talk to the Lord about any objections or reservations you have about this comparison.

❀ Allow the Holy Spirit to speak words of affirmation to you. Record anything that He brings to your mind as you are praying and listening.

Day 27: You Have a Secure Future

She laughs at the time to come. {Proverbs 31:25}

Here is a verse with so much meaning under the surface! The word *laughs* can be interpreted as *plays, jests, makes merry or rejoices*.[11] The Proverbs 31 woman is not worried about the future. She has made all preparations within her control and has left the rest to God. While she waits for the Lord's plans to unfold, she is living a life of joy.

We are called to lay down worry, especially over things that are out of our control. I heard a pastor say many years ago that, "If you know how to worry, then you know how to pray." It's a matter of taking the thing we are thinking about and lifting it to God in prayer, repeatedly if necessary. The Lord has already shown us that He has the future well in hand:

" *This is what the Lord says: "When seventy years are completed for Babylon, I will come to you and fulfill my good promise to bring you back to this place. For I know the plans I have for you," declares the Lord, "**plans to prosper you and not to harm you, plans to give you hope and a future**. Then you will call on me and come and pray to me, and I will listen to you. You will seek me and find me when you seek me with all your heart. I will be found by you," declares the Lord, "and will bring you back from captivity. Jeremiah 29:10-14*

God declares here His plans for His people, who were going to a foreign land for 70 years. They are asked to trust God, believe in His promises, and seek Him in the waiting. We are called to do the same.

The secret to rejoicing over the future is *full* and *flexible* trust in God and His promises. Putting our *full* trust in Him means that we don't trust in anything outside of God. This takes a great deal of practice. You may catch yourself relying on something other than Him—don't worry! You have the opportunity to pivot in that very moment and turn your eyes back to God.

A *flexible* trust is required when His plans take unexpected turns and delays. It's common for us to imagine what His promises will look like when fulfilled. We must be flexible when they turn out differently than we envisioned and commit to trusting God in the unexpected direction we are headed.

We have no guarantees in this life other than God's steady character as a faithful, loving Father. The Israelites had a time frame of 70 years, but more often than not, we don't even get time frames when it comes to the circumstances of our lives! We have to put our full trust in the Lord and lay down our desire to know and control the details.

Remember that God says:
I know the plans I have for you.

He does **not** say:
You know the plans I have for you.
You can see how the plans I have for you will work out.
You can predict the timeline of the plans I have for you.

The specifics of His plans are not our business until they come to pass. We know these plans are prosperous, generous, hopeful, purposeful, timely, and good! Even if the plans are not what we would choose for ourselves, we trust that God knows best.

❧ What concerns do you have about the future? Talk to the Lord about these.

❧ Ask the Lord to give you a verse or a prayer to hold on to, one that boosts your faith in His goodness and His perfect plans. If the Holy Spirit whispers a phrase to you, it might be from Scripture. If you're not sure if it's a verse, enter the phrase into Google search on your phone or computer and find out!

Day 28: You Walk in Joy

She laughs at the time to come. {Proverbs 31:25}

Let's spend another day talking about this verse. I used to laugh and rejoice over *my* imaginings and hopes for the future, but not when I thought about leaving all the decisions to the Lord. I honestly thought that I couldn't be happy unless I agreed to the plans! In one season several years ago, I felt led to deliberately allow the Lord to choose more things for me. I refrained from giving my opinions. I stopped considering whether I would like a certain thing or not. It was such a growing season for me! God selected some things that I would never have chosen for myself, and I discovered that I could love what God planned for me no matter what it was.

The best preparation for the unknown future is to make our hearts ready to trust Him no matter what. We do not need to know all the answers or details to be happy. We do not need to be in control to be at peace, nor do we need to be assured of any outcomes to experience joy.

It is possible to take the energy we formerly expended for worry and control, and instead invest it into building our trust in His goodness. One of the best building tools is confessing our lack of trust and our desire to trust more.

I found it beneficial to have some default prayers to pray when worry, analyzing, or controlling starts to creep in. When they are short and easy to memorize, practiced prayers can be very effective. With use, they become automatic when we don't know what to pray, or when we want to argue with God about the way things are going. I'll share some examples with the Scriptures that inspired each one.

"I put my trust in You, Lord."

❝ *In you, Lord my God, I put my trust. I trust in you; do not let me be put to shame, nor let my enemies triumph over me. No one who hopes in you will ever be put to shame.   Psalm 25:1-3*

"Increase my faith and trust in You, Lord."

❝ *(The boy's father said to Jesus), "...If you can do anything, take pity on us and help us."   "If you can?" said Jesus. "Everything is possible for one who believes." Immediately the boy's father exclaimed, "I do believe; help me overcome my unbelief!" Mark 9:22-24*

❝ *The apostles said to the Lord, "Increase our faith!" He replied, "If you have faith as small as a mustard seed, you can say to this mulberry tree, 'Be uprooted and planted in the sea,' and it will obey you." Luke 17:5-6*

"Show me the joy of trusting in You."

❝ *You are my God; have mercy on me, Lord, for I call to you all day long.   Bring joy to your servant, Lord, for I put my trust in you. Psalm 86:3-4*

❝ *May the God of hope fill you with all joy and peace as you trust in him, so that you may overflow with hope by the power of the Holy Spirit.   Romans 15:13*

Faith and trust are spiritual muscles that get stronger when they are exercised! When we use these muscles daily in the little things of life, our strengthened faith and trust work well when hard times come. We can truly rejoice, knowing that our future is in the hands of a God that we fully trust.

🌀 What gets in the way of you fully trusting the Lord? Talk to Him about this.

🌀 Close your eyes and imagine yourself standing before your future, allowing your imagination to create a scene in your mind.

🌀 Imagine Jesus is there with you. What interactions do you have there with Him?

🌀 Describe any joy that you felt.

Day 29: You Are Wise

She opens her mouth with wisdom. {Proverbs 31:26}

Even though several different Hebrew words translate to *wisdom*, the one used here for the Proverbs 31 woman is the same one that Solomon used when he famously asked God for wisdom:

❝ *That night God appeared to Solomon and said to him, "Ask for whatever you want me to give you." Solomon answered God, "You have shown great kindness to David my father and have made me king in his place. Now, Lord God, let your promise to my father David be confirmed, for you have made me king over a people who are as numerous as the dust of the earth. Give me* **wisdom** *and knowledge, that I may lead this people, for who is able to govern this great people of yours?"*

God said to Solomon, "Since this is your heart's desire and you have not asked for wealth, possessions or honor, nor for the death of your enemies, and since you have not asked for a long life but for wisdom and knowledge to govern my people over whom I have made you king, therefore **wisdom** *and knowledge will be given you. And I will also give you wealth, possessions, and honor, such as no king who was before you ever had and none after you will have."*   *2 Chronicles 1: 7-12*

Wisdom is more practical than theoretical. Wisdom goes beyond knowledge, insight, and experience. It is the ability to take information and insight and *put them into practice for the best outcome*.[12] Solomon asked for wisdom to lead God's people, in peacetime and wartime, on holy days and ordinary days, in times of famine and times of plenty.

The Hebrew word for wisdom in Proverbs 31 is not only used in Solomon's prayer, but also in this prophecy about Jesus:

*" A shoot will come up from the stump of Jesse; from his roots a Branch will bear fruit. The Spirit of the Lord will rest on him— the Spirit of **wisdom** and of understanding, the Spirit of counsel and of might, the Spirit of the knowledge and fear of the Lord—and he will delight in the fear of the Lord.   Isaiah 11:1-3a*

You and I have access to the same kind of wisdom that Solomon had because it came from the Spirit of the Lord who lives in us. I find that *wisdom flows when I pause.* As soon as I realize that a decision must be made, or that particular words need to be spoken, it's time to pause and let the Holy Spirit work. Sometimes I realize too late that I needed God's wisdom in a situation. I continue to recognize the depth of my need for God's wisdom to lead, to speak, and to carry out His plans in my midst.

I'll never forget the night that my husband went out for a guys' night with church friends. It was a short time after he had been in a serious auto accident. I cried myself to sleep that night after telling God that the man who walked out the door was not the man that I had married six years before. He'd been irritable, unable to sleep, and having fits of anger over little things. I asked God to show me what to do. At some point after midnight, I woke to the sound of the door opening as my husband arrived home. In that first second of wakefulness, the Holy Spirit whispered to my mind, "It's the medication he is taking."

The next morning, I shared with my husband the words of wisdom that God had revealed. We collected the bottles of medication that had been prescribed both by his regular doctor, and the hospital physician after his car accident, and did a little research. Sure enough, two of the medications should not have been prescribed together, and the result was insomnia and anxiety.

What a breakthrough that wisdom gave us! The Spirit of God always knows things that we do not. He is thoroughly acquainted with the past, the present, the future, and the full will of God. The best part is that His wisdom is accessible to us when we need it.

✤ Do you need wisdom for something specific right now? Talk to the Lord about it.

✤ What kind of situations in your life regularly require wisdom, for yourself or others?

✤ Ask the Lord to help you desire and seek His wisdom.

Day 30: You Are Kind

Kind instruction is on her tongue. {Proverbs 31:26}

The Proverbs 31 woman's words are governed by the law of *hesed*, the Hebrew word that is translated as *kindness, lovingkindness,* or *mercy*.[13] She loves, teaches, and counsels by God's law of mercy. This same word is used here in Lamentations:

" *Through the Lord's* **mercies***, we are not consumed, because His compassions fail not. They are new every morning; Great is Your faithfulness. "The Lord is my portion," says my soul, "Therefore I hope in Him!"*   *Lamentations 3:22-24 (NKJV)*

Mercy is kindness or leniency that is undeserved, given by someone who has the power to condemn or punish the recipient. God's mercy in this passage is very powerful—it keeps you and me from being consumed or destroyed by sin and shame. His mercies do not run out, because He has renewed compassion for us every day of our lives. Kindness for every failure. Mercy for every sin. Lovingkindness for every broken thing you've done out of your brokenness. Mercy right now, for you.

✿ Hover on that for a moment. What is your response to God's mercy and kindness?

Acts of kindness and mercy are tangible evidence of love and compassion. God has shown mercy to you so that, having a taste and an experience of it, you will be able to show the same to those around you. The woman in Proverbs 31 is doing just that. When she shows mercy to a child who disobeys, she is demonstrating God's forgiveness. When she shows kindness to a loved one who betrayed her, she is sharing that which God has poured out on her. When she shows mercy to the one who made a snap judgment or decision, she is sharing a taste of God's lovingkindness.

❧ Think of a time when you received a great act of kindness or mercy from someone. What impact did it have on you?

In the middle of our current "cancel culture", mercy is a rare gift given among people. You are a rare gift-giver. The Holy Spirit of God will move within you when He wants to extend his mercy to another through you. We cannot orchestrate these moments on our own, we must wait and watch as the Lord weaves our lives together and plants us in the mercy-giving seat in His timing.

" While Jesus was having dinner at Matthew's house, many tax collectors and sinners came and ate with him and his disciples. When the Pharisees saw this, they asked his disciples, "Why does your teacher eat with tax collectors and sinners?"

On hearing this, Jesus said, "It is not the healthy who need a doctor, but the sick. But go and learn what this means: 'I desire mercy, not sacrifice.' For I have not come to call the righteous, but sinners." Matthew 9:10-13

✿ Where do you need mercy today? Ask the Lord for it, or ask Him to show you where He is already trying to give it to you. Stay here a moment; don't rush.

✿ Who in your life needs kindness or mercy today? Let the Holy Spirit lead you. This is not a "should" or a "have to". God might use you to extend His love to someone today.

Day 31: You Watch Over Others

She looks well to the ways of her household. {Proverbs 31:27}

This verb *looks well* means to *watch, look out, spy, or observe.*[14] Just as Biblical settlements and towns employed towers with watchmen to observe anyone or anything unsafe that might approach, God has set women to keep an eye on their loved ones. Are you observant? Intuitive? Do you "just know" when something is up? That's God's design.

As a mother, I've received many nudges from the Holy Spirit to check on one of my children. The Lord has been faithful to give me a clue when one of them was experiencing trouble, a hurting heart, or unspoken anxiety. I've tried to be faithful in following through on these nudges because occasionally my intervention has been an answer to my kids' prayers. They didn't know they were praying for me to get involved; they were just asking the Lord to get them out of sticky situations or get some support. What a privilege to be an answer to prayer.

When we are watching over our friends and loved ones, we can observe many things. *It's important to know what to do with these observations.* Sometimes we are just called to pray and not say a thing! On other occasions, we are led to confront or challenge. Sometimes we are appointed to be a peacemaker. Many situations require us to be the hands, feet, and voice of Jesus.

" Unless the Lord builds the house, the builders labor in vain. Unless the Lord watches over the city, the guards stand watch in vain. Psalm 127:1

Beware of your default responses and let God lead, otherwise, the watching is in vain. It's so easy to worry, to criticize, to try to control, or to shame instead of pausing to let the Holy Spirit guide our next steps. God will often be more focused on what's happening *inside* the person rather than what is seen on the *outside*. So much of our sin and failure is linked to our brokenness! We often act out because of our pain, fear, or need for control, and that is likely what our loved ones are doing when we see something amiss in their behavior. God wants to get to the heart of the matter to bring healing and freedom. We must stand by for His guidance and hold loosely to the person or the situation so that He can do the work He wants to do.

" With a loud cry, Jesus breathed his last. The curtain of the temple was torn in two from top to bottom. And when the centurion, who stood there in front of Jesus, saw how he died, he said, "Surely this man was the Son of God!"

Some women were watching from a distance. Among them were Mary Magdalene, Mary the mother of James the younger and Joseph, and Salome. In Galilee, these women had followed him and cared for his needs. Many other women who had come up with him to Jerusalem were also there. Mark 15:37-41

Even Jesus had women watching over Him, caring for Him. What a holy ministry *watching* can be! Keeping an eye on loved ones makes us invested. It gives us powerful insight for praying. With the guidance of the Holy Spirit, we can participate in the work that God is doing around us.

✿ Who have you been watching over?

❁ Ask the Lord to show you what He wants you to do for these loved ones.

❁ Is anyone watching over you (besides God)?

❁ Talk to the Lord about this. Do you need to allow or invite anyone to watch over you?

Day 32: You Need Rest

(She) doesn't eat the bread of idleness. {Proverbs 31:27}

❧ What comes to mind when you think of idleness or idling?

Biblical idleness has been defined as *not employed; unoccupied with business; inactive; doing nothing, averse to labor; lazy; unfruitful; barren; not productive of good.*[15] Being idle means being inactive when activity is needed. However, this is not a mandate to busy ourselves around the clock. While the Bible does not approve of idling, it does encourage a balance of work and rest.

" *It is in vain that you rise up early and go late to rest, eating the bread of anxious toil; for he gives to his beloved sleep.*
Psalm 127:2 (ESV)

How can we tell the difference between being idle and resting? Idleness may be a way of procrastinating or escaping from problems or difficult circumstances in our lives. Sometimes we want to "check out" from the things that are causing us stress.

Rest, on the other hand, is an opportunity to lay down the problems or difficult circumstances, knowing that they will be there when our rest is over but also knowing that God will not stop working on our behalf while we are resting.

While rest is refreshing, idleness is not. There is nothing rewarding about avoiding what needs to be done and thinking negative thoughts about ourselves and our circumstances. On the contrary, I feel most alive after permitting rest and then re-engaging in the work that God has called me to.

Perhaps idleness comes when we need rest, but we don't allow ourselves to take time for it. We get stuck in the idle position, not having the energy or will for anything, yet shaming ourselves all the while about the things we "should be" doing. If we recognize our need for rest instead of fighting it, the frustration and idleness could give way to some health-restoring rest.

❧ Is idleness a problem for you? Consider whether you've permitted enough rest for yourself. Talk to the Lord about it.

" The apostles gathered around Jesus and reported to him all they had done and taught. Then, because so many people were coming and going that they did not even have a chance to eat, he said to them, "Come with me by yourselves to a quiet place and get some rest." So they went away by themselves in a boat to a solitary place. Mark 6:30-32

This interaction between Jesus and His disciples happened after they returned from a ministry adventure. Jesus had sent them out in pairs to preach the gospel, cast out evil spirits, and anoint and heal the sick. They came back both exhilarated and exhausted, and Jesus knew what they needed.

❧ Read Jesus' invitation in the previous passage from Mark. Is He calling you to "come with Me by yourself to a quiet place and get some rest"?

❧ Ask the Lord if He has any recommendations for you regarding rest.

Day 33: You Are Blessed

Her children rise up and call her blessed. {Proverbs 31:28}

People will call you many things in your life: blessed and otherwise! They may not call you mother, but they may call you sister, auntie, teacher, doctor, caregiver, mentor, neighbor, or godmother. Sadly, some may not call you the thing that you most want to be called. You may even be called a failure, a thief, a liar, a hypocrite, or the like. Perhaps they will not call you at all. Whatever it is, you cannot live by what others call you or say about you.

People will call you by titles and descriptors based on *their* perspectives and feelings. Some can be received and believed. Others need to be disregarded. Asking the Holy Spirit to be a filter for the things you hear from others is a good habit to practice.

❀ Is there something you long to be called? Write it down and talk to God about this.

❀ Have you been called something that wounds you to this day? Bring your wounds from words that have been spoken to you before the Lord. Record any insights you get from Him.

Now, the most important question: What does God call you?

" *I no longer call you servants, because a servant does not know his master's business. Instead,* **I have called you friends**, *for everything that I learned from my Father I have made known to you. (John 15:15).*

" *For we are God's* **masterpiece**. *He has created us anew in Christ Jesus, so we can do the good things he planned for us long ago. (Ephesians 2:10 NLT).*

" *For you are a people holy to the Lord your God. The Lord your God has chosen you out of all the peoples on the face of the earth to be his people,* **his treasured possession**. *(Deuteronomy 7:6).*

" *My* **beloved** *is mine and I am his (Song of Solomon 2:16).*

" *I will be a Father to you, and you will be my sons and* **daughters**, *says the Lord Almighty. (2 Corinthians 6:18).*

❀ Meditate on the verse above that stands out to you the most. What is God showing you?

❀ What is the Lord calling you today? Write down any words that come to mind. Let the Holy Spirit speak.

Day 34: You Are Excellent

Her husband also praises her... "Many women do noble things,
but you excel them all." {Proverbs 31:28b-29}

As we begin digging into these verses, let me remind you that
whether you are married, single, divorced, widowed, or in a
complicated relationship, *your Maker is your husband* (Isaiah
54:5). Take a minute to acknowledge that truth.

❀ What do you need from your Maker today?

❀ Pause for a bit and let Him speak to your heart. Let Him boast
and praise you if He wants to, as the husband in Proverbs 31
does. Record any important words here.

The Proverbs 31 woman is told that many of her kind have
lived virtuously, or valiantly, but she excels them all. What
incredible words! Remember that in verse 10 (day 4 of our
journey) we learned that this word *virtuous* is rich with military

meaning. Many women have been faithful warriors, but the Proverbs 31 woman has excelled them all.

As a recovering perfectionist and performer, this verse has always pushed me in an unhealthy way. I desired to excel but often went about it the wrong way. The drive within was to perform and be good enough for God (and others) to approve of me and value me, rather than a desire to let the Holy Spirit excel within me.

I recently discovered something interesting while studying the words in these verses. The Hebrew word *excel* means what one would expect: *to rise up, to ascend above, or to be exalted*. The human mind can easily translate that into "I must rise up. I must ascend above. I must work to be exalted." However, my perspective was drastically changed when I found a verse in the Psalms that uses the same word (*excel*) in a different way:

*" He **lifted me out** of the pit of despair, out of the mud and the mire. He set my feet on solid ground and steadied me as I walked along.   Psalm 40:2 (NLT)*

I was surprised to learn that *excel* can also mean *to go up, to be taken up, or to be drawn up.*[17] This suggests that the subject itself does not always ascend on its own, but that it can be drawn or carried up.

How often do we spin our wheels, wasting time and energy, trying to raise ourselves up and ascend to where we think we ought to be? How often are we unable to truly excel at something because we don't have the power to make it happen? Perhaps the key to excelling is to let God lift us up.

✥ What areas of your life have you tried to or desired to excel in?

✥ Bring these areas before the Lord and ask for His perspective. Jot down any insight you receive.

✥ In what ways do you need to be lifted to excel? Ask God to lift you up.

Day 35: You Are Favored

Charm is deceptive, *and beauty is vain, but a woman who fears Yahweh, she shall be praised. {Proverbs 31:30}*

The word *charm* in today's verse is better translated as *favor*. The way it is used here in Proverbs is unique, as most of the other uses in the Old Testament express favor found in someone's sight.[18] Here are some examples:

" *And He said, "My presence shall go with you, and I will give you rest." Then (Moses) said to Him, "If Your presence does not go with us, do not lead us up from here. For how then can it be known that I have found **favor in Your sight,** I and Your people? Is it not by Your going with us, so that we, I and Your people, may be distinguished from all the other people who are on the face of the earth?" Exodus 33:14-16 (NASB)*

" *When the king saw Esther the queen standing in the courtyard, she obtained **favor in his sight**; and the king extended to Esther the golden scepter which was in his hand. So Esther approached and touched the top of the scepter. Then the king said to her, "What is troubling you, Queen Esther? And what is your request? Up to half of the kingdom, it shall be given to you." Esther 5:2-3 (NASB)*

❀ The context of these passages seems to show the concept of favor in a positive light, so why do you think the writer of Proverbs would say that favor is deceptive?

❀ Have you ever found yourself working too hard to earn the favor of someone in your life?

The favor of people is a fickle thing. It is long and hard to earn, yet can be lost in a moment over the smallest of things. Let God establish your favor with people. Do not try to earn it yourself. It is a slippery slope and you will often lose yourself and your values trying to please others.

❝ *Do not let kindness and truth leave you; Bind them around your neck, write them on the tablet of your heart. So you will find* **favor** *and a good reputation* **in the sight of God and man**. *Trust in the Lord with all your heart and do not lean on your own understanding. In all your ways acknowledge Him, and He will make your paths straight. Proverbs 3:3-6 (NASB)*

❀ How have you experienced the favor of God in your life?

❀ Do you need more of His favor right now? Talk to the Lord about what you need.

Day 36: You Are Beautiful

*Charm is deceptive, **and beauty is vain**, but a woman who
fears Yahweh, she shall be praised. {Proverbs 31:30}*

✺ What do you think the phrase *beauty is vain* means? Take note
that the Hebrew word for *vain* translates literally as *a vapor* or *a
breath* that disappears momentarily.[19]

Physical beauty does not last forever. The outward features of
a woman change over time. The loveliness of a flower begins to
diminish the moment the stem is cut. The majesty of a sunset
disappears once twilight takes over. The beauty of a forest can be
swallowed up in moments by a fire.

We can spend our lives chasing beauty only to have it turn to
vapor before our eyes. Our bodies are prone to change, sickness
and aging, making the world's standard of beauty impossible to
achieve or sustain. In my pursuit of understanding God's standard
of beauty, I had to release the idea that my body, as the temple of
the Holy Spirit, must meet the world's standard of beauty and size
to be good enough. Nowhere in Scripture will you find a universal
mandate to pursue physical beauty or a particular body size.
Consider the following words written about Jesus by Isaiah the
prophet, hundreds of years before our Savior was born:

" He had no beauty or majesty to attract us to him, nothing in his appearance that we should desire him. He was despised and rejected by mankind, a man of suffering, and familiar with pain. Like one from whom people hide their faces he was despised, and we held him in low esteem. Surely he took up our pain and bore our suffering, yet we considered him punished by God, stricken by him, and afflicted.

But he was pierced for our transgressions, he was crushed for our iniquities, the punishment that brought us peace was on him, and by his wounds we are healed. We all, like sheep, have gone astray, each of us has turned to our own way; and the Lord has laid on him the iniquity of us all. Isaiah 53:2b-6

❀ What drew the multitudes to Jesus if it *wasn't* his appearance or charm?

" But the Lord said to Samuel, "Do not consider his appearance or his height, for I have rejected him. The Lord does not look at the things people look at. People look at the outward appearance, but the Lord looks at the heart." 1 Samuel 16:7

❀ What does this passage reveal about God's view of the physical appearance of His people?

❀ How does this affect your perception of your own beauty?

Day 37: You Honor God

Charm is deceptive, and beauty is vain, ***but a woman who fears Yahweh, she shall be praised.*** *{Proverbs 31:30}*

Let's focus on the last part of this verse today. We see a clear statement about what God values: a woman who fears or honors Him above worldly things. How contradictory to what the world values, with its daily input on what women ought to be! It is difficult to avoid getting bogged down in worries about our success, our favor with others, and our physical appearances.

I spent most of my adult life trying to make myself thinner and more beautiful to fit in. All those years that I longed to have a different body, what I was truly longing for was acceptance, approval, and love from others. The enemy had instilled this belief in me from an early age: not having an ideal appearance meant that I was unlovable and unworthy. The fear of being in a larger body drove me to seek control over how I appeared to others through dieting and exercise. Sadly, I even spiritualized my obsession, thinking God would approve of me more if I was a smaller size.

I invested tremendous energy in my physical appearance, food consumption, and exercise. Why was this the primary drive in my life? Was I fearing the Lord, or was I fearing rejection based on my appearance?

The funny thing is that I already had so much of what I deeply longed for: family and friends who thought me beautiful inside and out, plus a heavenly Father who adored me and valued me no matter what I looked like. Once I let go of the fears and truly recognized how loved and accepted I already was, I was finally free to worship the Lord with all of my heart, mind, soul, and strength.

❧ Is there something holding you back from fearing and worshiping the Lord with your whole being?

❧ Talk to the Lord about what is getting in the way. Record any encouragement He gives you.

Consider the woman in the next passage, who set aside all thoughts of societal rules and material things when she crashed a dinner party to worship Jesus:

" While he was in Bethany, reclining at the table in the home of Simon the Leper, a woman came with an alabaster jar of very expensive perfume, made of pure nard. She broke the jar and poured the perfume on his head. Some of those present were saying indignantly to one another, "Why this waste of perfume? It could have been sold for more than a year's wages and the money given to the poor." And they rebuked her harshly.

"Leave her alone," said Jesus. "Why are you bothering her? She has done a beautiful thing to me. The poor you will always have with you, and you can help them any time you want. But you *will not always have me. She did what she could. She poured perfume on my body beforehand to prepare for my burial. Truly I tell you, wherever the gospel is preached throughout the world, what she has done will also be told, in memory of her." Mark 14:3-9*

She expressed her awe and love for Jesus in a way that was contrary to the world's expectations of women. She was a woman who feared the Lord and she was praised for it, both in the moment and for all time.

🌀 Close your eyes and imagine that you are somewhere alone with Jesus. Express your devotion to Him in some way, in the manner you feel led. If nothing comes to mind, imagine yourself anointing Him with oil the way the woman did in the gospel passage. Record any memorable moments or insights here.

Day 38: Your Fruit Will Last

Give her of the fruit of her hands. {Prov 31:31}

It's no surprise that a Proverbs 31 woman reaps what she sows. That means you, too! We can enjoy the fruit of the hard work and devotion we employ in our lives. We may see fruit from personal spiritual growth, profit from enterprises at home or at work, fruit from ministry endeavors, or growth and fulfillment from relationship investments. Our work is not in vain.

🌀 What fruit have you enjoyed in your life so far?

🌀 What fruit has been the most rewarding?

For me, the fruit of trusting fully in God has been the sweetest and most surprising of any fruit I've tasted. I had no idea how much joy and peace I would experience if I could manage to completely trust in the Lord and stop analyzing, controlling, and performing. I used to experience what I *thought* was joy and peace, but it turned out to be very conditional. It was only when I felt in control of my life—either through seeing, knowing, or deciding what was coming next—that I felt happy. I had no idea that this "happiness" would pale in comparison to the joy of completely letting go and knowing that God has me in his capable hands, even in great circumstantial uncertainty or suffering.

This fruit that came from laying down self-sufficiency and the need for control has been more satisfying than any of the accomplishments I achieved working on my own to please God. I thought my life would spin out if I gave up the steering wheel. In my head, I knew that God was "in control", but I had assigned way too much personal responsibility to myself. I had so many "to-do" items on my list and felt that it was up to me to steer a life that pleased God. What a relief to let go and let God truly lead, supply, and decide what was best for me.

It is possible to be so busy producing and harvesting the fruit of our choosing that we miss out on the fruit that God wants to bring about in our lives. We can be so consumed with deciding what kind of fruit would most please Him, that we aren't aware of where He might be trying to lead us. It's time to stop, lay down our ideas and agendas, and wait to see what He has planned next. The seed that He plants, tends, prunes, and harvests will be far more satisfying than any fruit we can imagine.

" Very truly I tell you, unless a kernel of wheat falls to the ground and dies, it remains only a single seed. But if it dies, it produces many seeds. Anyone who loves their life will lose it, while anyone who hates their life in this world will keep it for eternal life. Whoever serves me must follow me; and where I am, my servant also will be. My Father will honor the one who serves me. John 12:24-26

✥ Ask the Lord to show you what fruit pleases Him most in your life. Resist the urge to *assume* what He will say and just wait for the Lord to give you a word, a picture, a memory, or a verse to show you.

✥ Now ask the Lord if there is another kind of fruit He would like to bear in you. Again, no assumptions. Lay them down. Wait for Him to show you.

Day 39: You Shall Be Praised

Let her works praise her in the gates! {Proverbs 31:31}

This is the third time the Proverbs 31 writer declares that an excellent, fruitful, God-fearing woman is worthy of praise. Not just at home, but also at the community gates. Nothing else (except various references to her hands) is repeated as many times as the call for praise.

*Her husband also **praises** her, "Many women do noble things, but you excel them all." (v. 28-29)*

*A woman who fears Yahweh, she shall be **praised**. (v. 30)*

*Let her works **praise** her in the gates! (v. 31)*

❀ What do you think about this emphasis on praise for us as women?

❀ Can we conclude that God wants us to receive praise?

Both the husband and wife are known "at the city gates" and are respected in the community. There is an indication of equality here, which seems remarkable, considering how the Hebrew culture generally limited women in their opportunities and rights. Though their roles were different, both the man and the woman in this passage positively influenced their community and were honored for it.

Just as the woman in the passage was highly esteemed at home, in her social circles, and by her Heavenly Father, YOU are also highly esteemed. Your work and devotion do not go unnoticed. You matter. Your care for others, the light you radiate, and the unique work you do are important. God sees, and He is inclined to praise you for it.

❝ *"His master replied, 'Well done, good and faithful servant! You have been faithful with a few things; I will put you in charge of many things. Come and share your master's happiness!' Matthew 25:21*

Of course, we can do nothing truly good without God's guidance and the power of the Holy Spirit, so we give Him the glory for the things He is accomplishing through us.

❝ *Now may the God of peace, who through the blood of the eternal covenant brought back from the dead our Lord Jesus, that great Shepherd of the sheep, equip you with everything good for doing his will, and may he work in us what is pleasing to him, through Jesus Christ, to whom be glory forever and ever. Amen. Hebrews 13:20-21*

❀ Take a moment to sit quietly with the Lord. Allow Him to speak any words of affirmation or gratitude to you. You might feel some resistance to this idea, but try to let go and see what the Holy Spirit might whisper to you.

❀ Respond to God's praise.

Day 40: Final Reflection

" Who can find a worthy woman?
For her price is far above rubies.
The heart of her husband trusts in her.
He shall have no lack of gain.
She does him good, not harm, all the days of her life.
She seeks wool and flax, and works eagerly with her hands.
She is like the merchant ships.
She brings her bread from afar.
She rises also while it is yet night, gives food to her household, and portions for her servant girls.
She considers a field and buys it.
With the fruit of her hands, she plants a vineyard.
She arms her waist with strength, and makes her arms strong.
She perceives that her merchandise is profitable.
Her lamp doesn't go out by night.
She lays her hands to the distaff, and her hands hold the spindle.
She opens her arms to the poor; yes, she extends her hands to the needy.
She is not afraid of the snow for her household; for all her household are clothed with scarlet.
She makes for herself carpets of tapestry.
Her clothing is fine linen and purple.
Her husband is respected in the gates, when he sits among the elders of the land.
She makes linen garments and sells them, and delivers sashes to the merchant.
Strength and dignity are her clothing.
She laughs at the time to come.
She opens her mouth with wisdom.
Kind instruction is on her tongue.

She looks well to the ways of her household, and doesn't eat the bread of idleness.
Her children rise up and call her blessed.
Her husband also praises her: "Many women do noble things, but you excel them all."
Charm is deceitful, and beauty is vain; but a woman who fears Yahweh, she shall be praised.
Give her of the fruit of her hands!
Let her works praise her in the gates!

✥ What has been the greatest blessing of this 40-day journey?

✥ What new insights have been helpful?

✥ Did the Lord answer any objections or questions from day 3?

❀ In what ways have you felt affirmed by God as you read through Proverbs 31 with new eyes?

❀ Do you sense some new work that the Lord is doing in you?

Endnotes

[1] Evans, Rachel Held. "3 Things You Might Not Know About Proverbs 31". *Rachel Held Evans Blog.* May 12, 2014. www.rachelheldevans.com/blog/3-things-you-might-not-know-about-proverbs-31

[2] "H2428 - ḥayil - Strong's Hebrew Lexicon (KJV)." Blue Letter Bible. Web. Retrieved 25 Oct., 2021. www.blueletterbible.org/lexicon/h2428/kjv/wlc/0-1/.

[3] "Sunrise Ruby." *Wikipedia*. Wikimedia Foundation. 5 July 2021. en.wikipedia.org/wiki/Sunrise_Ruby.

[4] "Definition of Strong". *Oxford University Press.* Lexico.com. Retrieved 15 October 2021. www.lexico.com/en/definition/strong.

[5] "H2938 - ṭāʿam - Strong's Hebrew Lexicon (KJV)." Blue Letter Bible. Web. Retrieved 25 Oct., 2021. www.blueletterbible.org/lexicon/h2938/kjv/wlc/0-1/.

[6] FirstKnowThyself. "No one else is supposed to understand your calling." *Instagram*, 9 Feb. 2019, www.instagram.com/p/CLE-26lHSv1/?utm_medium=copy_link.

[7] Parsons, John J. "The Holy Menorah." *Hebrew for Christians*. www.hebrew4christians.com/Scripture/Parashah/Summaries/Tetzaveh/Menorah/menorah. Viewed 12 Aug. 2021

[8] "Distaff". *Wikipedia*. Wikimedia Foundation. 8 June 2021. en.wikipedia.org/wiki/Distaff.

[9] "H8336 - šēš - Strong's Hebrew Lexicon (KJV)." Blue Letter Bible. Web. Retrieved 25 Oct., 2021. www.blueletterbible.org/lexicon/h8336/kjv/wlc/0-1/.

[10] "Definition of Dignity." *Oxford University Press.* Lexico.com. Retrieved 20 October 2021. www.lexico.com/en/definition/dignity.

[11] "H7832 - śāḥaq - Strong's Hebrew Lexicon (KJV)." Blue Letter Bible. Web. Retrieved 25 Oct., 2021. www.blueletterbible.org/lexicon/h7832/kjv/wlc/0-1/.

[12] "Definition of Wisdom." *KJV Dictionary*. AV1611.com. Retrieved 25 Oct. 2021. www.av1611.com/kjbp/kjv-dictionary/wisdom.

[13] "H2617 - ḥeseḏ - Strong's Hebrew Lexicon (KJV)." Blue Letter Bible. Web. Retrieved 25 Oct., 2021. www.blueletterbible.org/lexicon/h2617/kjv/wlc/0-1/.

[14] "H6822 - ṣāp̄â - Strong's Hebrew Lexicon (KJV)." Blue Letter Bible. Web. Retrieved 25 Oct., 2021. www.blueletterbible.org/lexicon/h6822/kjv/wlc/0-1/.

[15] "Definition of Idle." *KJV Dictionary*. AV1611.com. Retrieved 12 Sept. 2021. www.av1611.com/kjbp/kjv-dictionary/idle

[16] Douglass, Judy. "The Names God Calls Me." *Judy Douglass Blog*. 6 Mar. 2013. www.judydouglass.com/blog/2013/03/the-names-god-calls-me.

[17] "H5927 - ʿālâ - Strong's Hebrew Lexicon (KJV)." Blue Letter Bible. Web. Retrieved 25 Oct., 2021. www.blueletterbible.org/lexicon/h5927/kjv/wlc/0-1/.

[18] "H2580 - ḥēn - Strong's Hebrew Lexicon (KJV)." Blue Letter Bible. Web. Retrieved 25 Oct., 2021. www.blueletterbible.org/lexicon/h2580/kjv/wlc/0-1/.

[19] "H1892 - heḇel - Strong's Hebrew Lexicon (KJV)." Blue Letter Bible. Web. Retrieved 25 Oct., 2021. <https://www.blueletterbible.org/lexicon/h1892/kjv/wlc/0-1/>.

How Can I Be Saved?

How can I know that I am going to Heaven? Is this necessary? What does it mean to follow Jesus? You may have many questions, and I will do my best to answer with God's own words from the Bible.

" *Jesus said, "Very truly I tell you, no one can see the kingdom of God unless they are born again." John 3:3*

" *All praise to God, the Father of our Lord Jesus Christ. It is by his great mercy that we have been born again, because God raised Jesus Christ from the dead. Now we live with great expectation, and we have a priceless inheritance—an inheritance that is kept in heaven for you, pure and undefiled, beyond the reach of change and decay." 1 Peter 1:3-4 NLT*

The book of Romans in the New Testament lays out some clear guidelines regarding being born again and receiving salvation:

" *It is written: "There is no one righteous, not even one..." Romans 3:10*

" *...for all have sinned and fall short of the glory of God, and all are justified freely by his grace through the redemption that came by Christ Jesus. God presented Christ as a sacrifice of atonement, through the shedding of his blood—to be received by faith. He did this to demonstrate his righteousness, because in his forbearance he had left the sins committed beforehand unpunished." Romans 3:23-25*

" *...the wages of sin is death, but the gift of God is eternal life in Christ Jesus our Lord." Romans 6:23*

"If you declare with your mouth, "Jesus is Lord," and believe in your heart that God raised him from the dead, you will be saved. For it is with your heart that you believe and are justified, and it is with your mouth that you profess your faith and are saved. As Scripture says, "Anyone who believes in him will never be put to shame...for, "Everyone who calls on the name of the Lord will be saved." Romans 10:9-11, 13

It's clear that God does this work in us, as we can do nothing to save ourselves.

" For it is by grace you have been saved, through faith—and this is not from yourselves, it is the gift of God— not by works, so that no one can boast." Ephesians 2:8-9

I have no doubt that Jesus has used this devotional book to do what He talked about in the following verses:

" Jesus said, "Here I am! I stand at the door and knock. If anyone hears my voice and opens the door, I will come in and dine with that person, and they with me. Revelation 3:20

If He is knocking at the door of your heart, I pray that you will let Him in. You can do that easily with a prayer like this:

Jesus, I know that I have sinned and fallen short of both your glory and the person you made me to be. I recognize that you created me and that You have a plan for my life. Thank you for paying the penalty for my sins by dying on the cross. I ask your forgiveness for all that I've done. I accept the cleansing and grace you have promised to those who believe. Please come in, I am opening the door to my heart and my life. I want you to be my Lord and Savior. Help me to understand all that I am praying and asking. Show me the way from here and help me to find others who can help me grow in my new life with You. Amen.

Made in the USA
Middletown, DE
22 November 2021

52834081R00088